ATTACHMENTS

PHOTOGRAPHS

ANNE-MARIE COTTENET DANNENBERG

www.aavabooks.com

First Edition

Design by Leena Mast-Knutar

Printed in Finland by Art-Print Oy
Helsinki 2006

ISBN 952-5490-10-6

CONTENTS

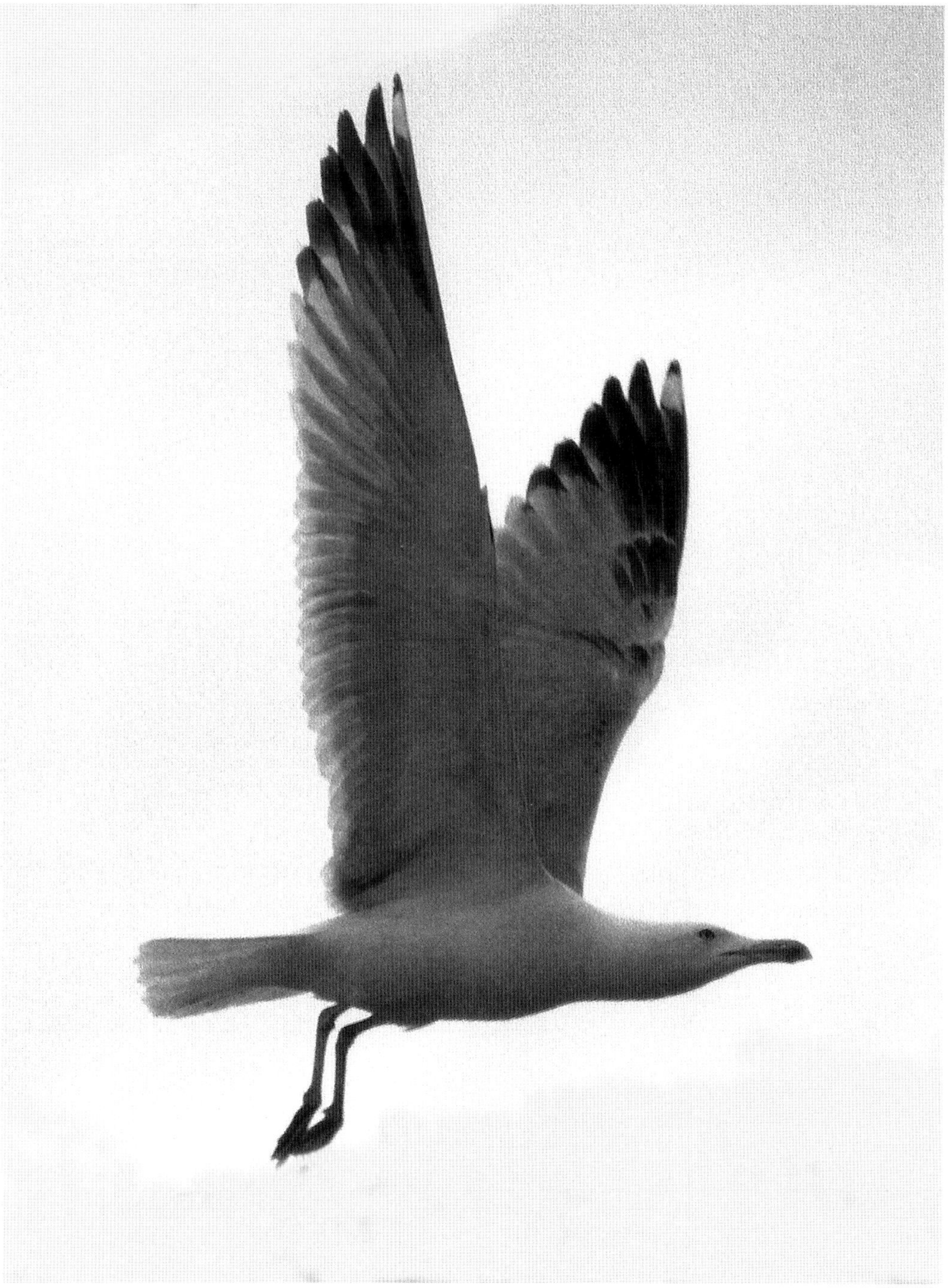

INTRODUCTION

The idea of this book came up after I noticed an older couple that was waiting at the same bus stop on the upper westside of Manhattan, a few years ago. The woman was wearing an unusually large, heart-shaped rhinestone pin. I wondered about this pin, what it meant to her, what interesting story was behind it.

For days I kept thinking of this pin. This is when I decided I would ask my family, friends, and acquaintances if they had an object that they strongly cherished. If they were willing to share the story behind it, I would photograph them and the object. A short text was to accompany the photographs.

Many of the chosen objects are anchored in the past. They may be connected to a specific person, a group of persons, or humanity in general. Some recall childhood events. Some are "objects" of inspiration, creation or appreciation. Their sizes vary from that of a tiny object to the immensity of the ocean. They all carry an emotional weight.

In this book the participants are from different countries, come from diverse backgrounds and cultures. For many of them English is not the main language... A few among them are well known, but most of them are people like you and me and not celebrities. This is what I chose... As the project evolved, it became richer in significance. For all of us it has been a voyage of discovery.

So here is a book to encourage those who read it to take the time to recognize those "things" that time and love have invested with meaning, a meaning that too often has been buried beneath our daily restlessness.

Anne-Marie Cottenet Dannenberg

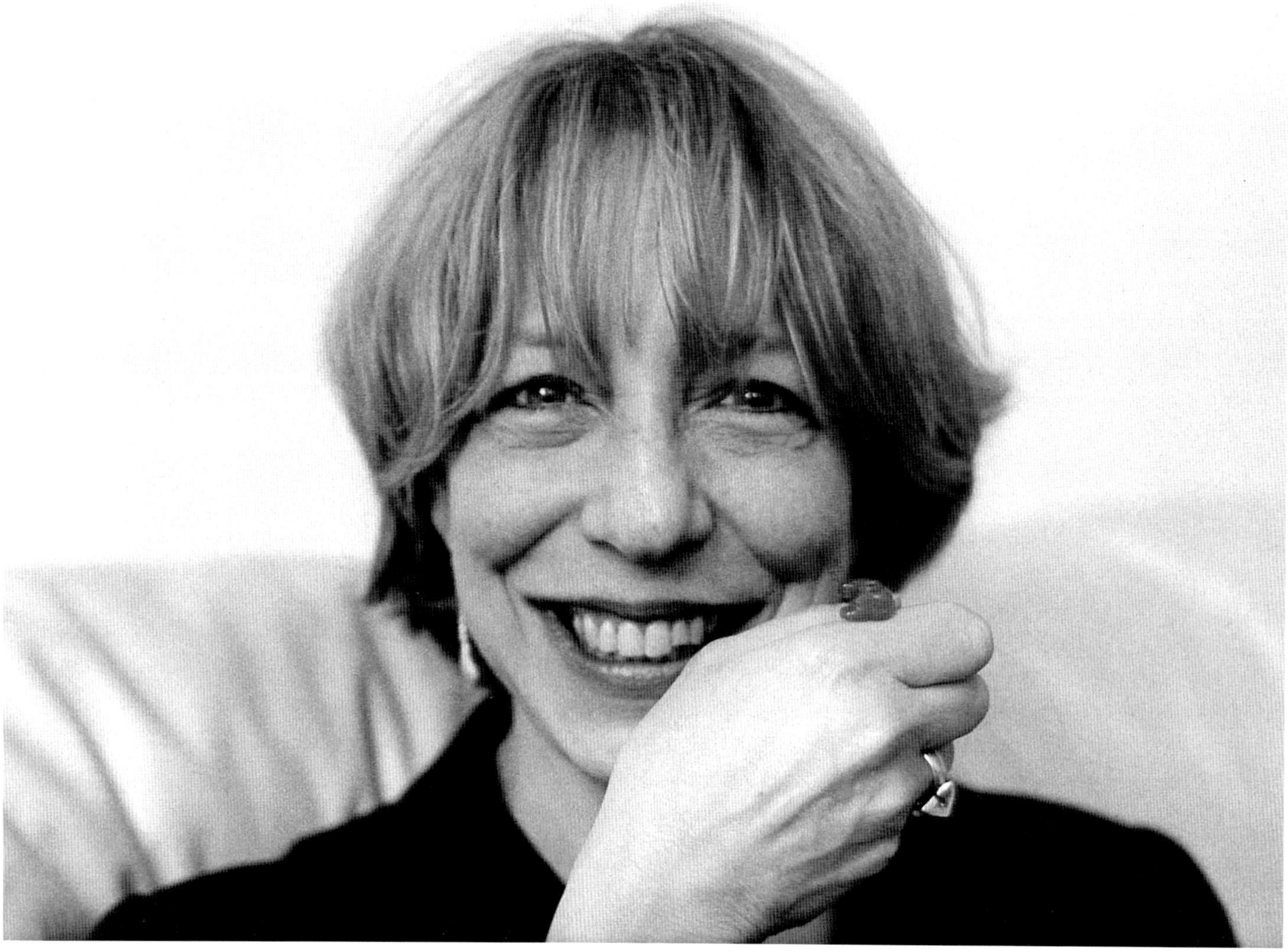

THE CARNELIAN BUNNY

About eight years ago, on a whim, I bought a very small carnelian bunny. My affection for unusual images of rabbits and bunnies has persisted since childhood, and I love the luminous color of this particular stone. From the beginning I thought of this object as a talisman, with special properties, and upon learning that in certain American Indian mythology it symbolizes facing your deepest fears, it became even more special to me. When a close friend of mine became ill and was facing a difficult surgery, I gave her my bunny – with the caveat that she must return it to me when she was well. Since that time, this little bunny has become a world traveler. It has seen friends through difficult journeys and hard times, sometimes health-related, sometimes personal. With each situation, when it returns to me, it takes on greater significance. And when it is not on loan taking care of someone I love, it lives with me.

Fran Kaufman
Art Dealer

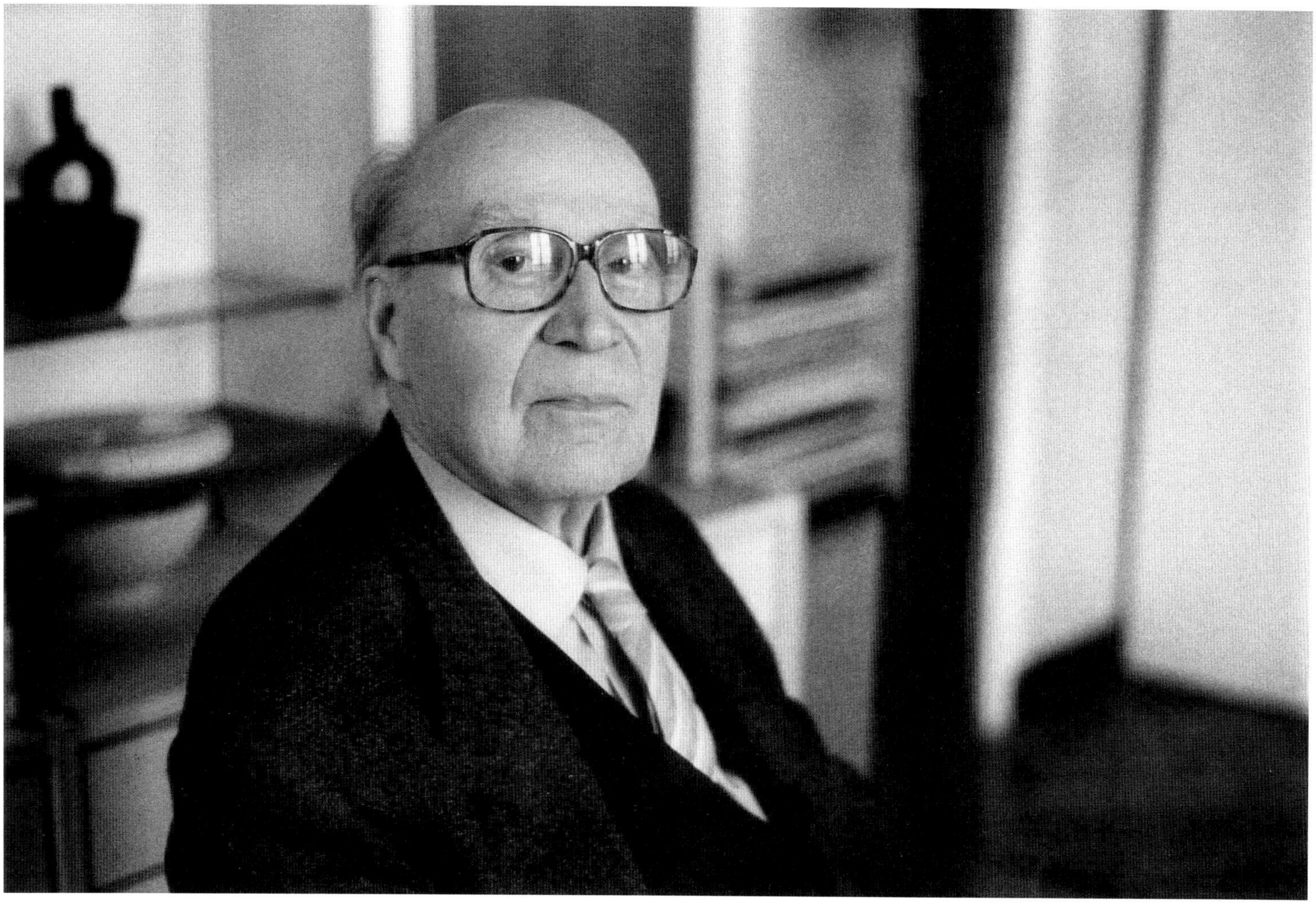

THE GOLD RING

This small gold ring is for me a quite precious object. It remains the only concrete symbol of a ceremony which took place more than a quarter of a century ago, and leaves me with only vague memories.

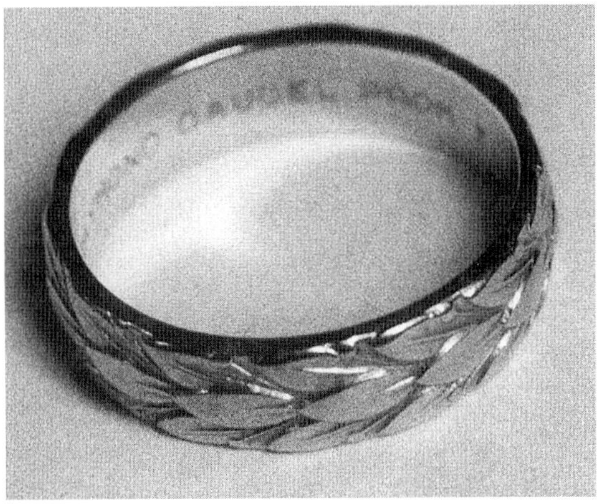

During this ceremony in Upsala, the former capital of Sweden, I was given my first Doctor Honoris Causa title in the presence of His Majesty the King of Sweden, in the form of a crown of laurels deposited on my head and this ring.

Raymond Daudel
Chemistry Professor
President of European Academy of Arts
Sciences and Letters

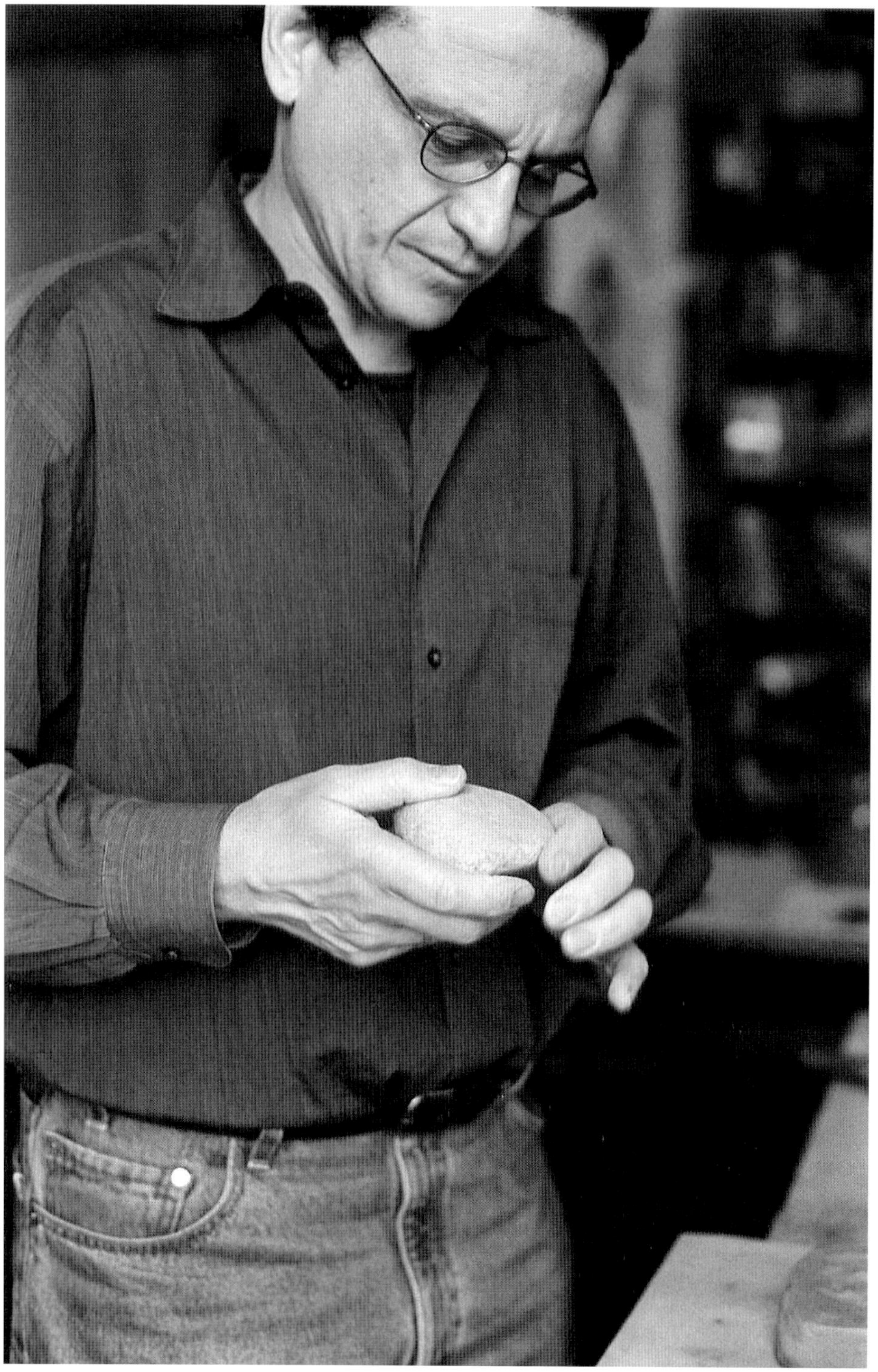

THE STONE

Objects can be magic.

Like friends, they choose us as much as we choose them.

Julius' shirt made on Saville Row and worn to threads. Dr. Bird's hat, a ladder, a teapot, a knife, a silk scarf.

These are the things I wanted to be photographed with. Most are gone, used up in time.

And then I thought of the stone.

On Monhegan Island, while preparing for a show, I picked it up. I use it to gouge out the metal of my etching plates and hack out marks in the clay. Most of the time, while working, I don't even know it's there.

Harold Wortsman
Printmaker / Sculptor

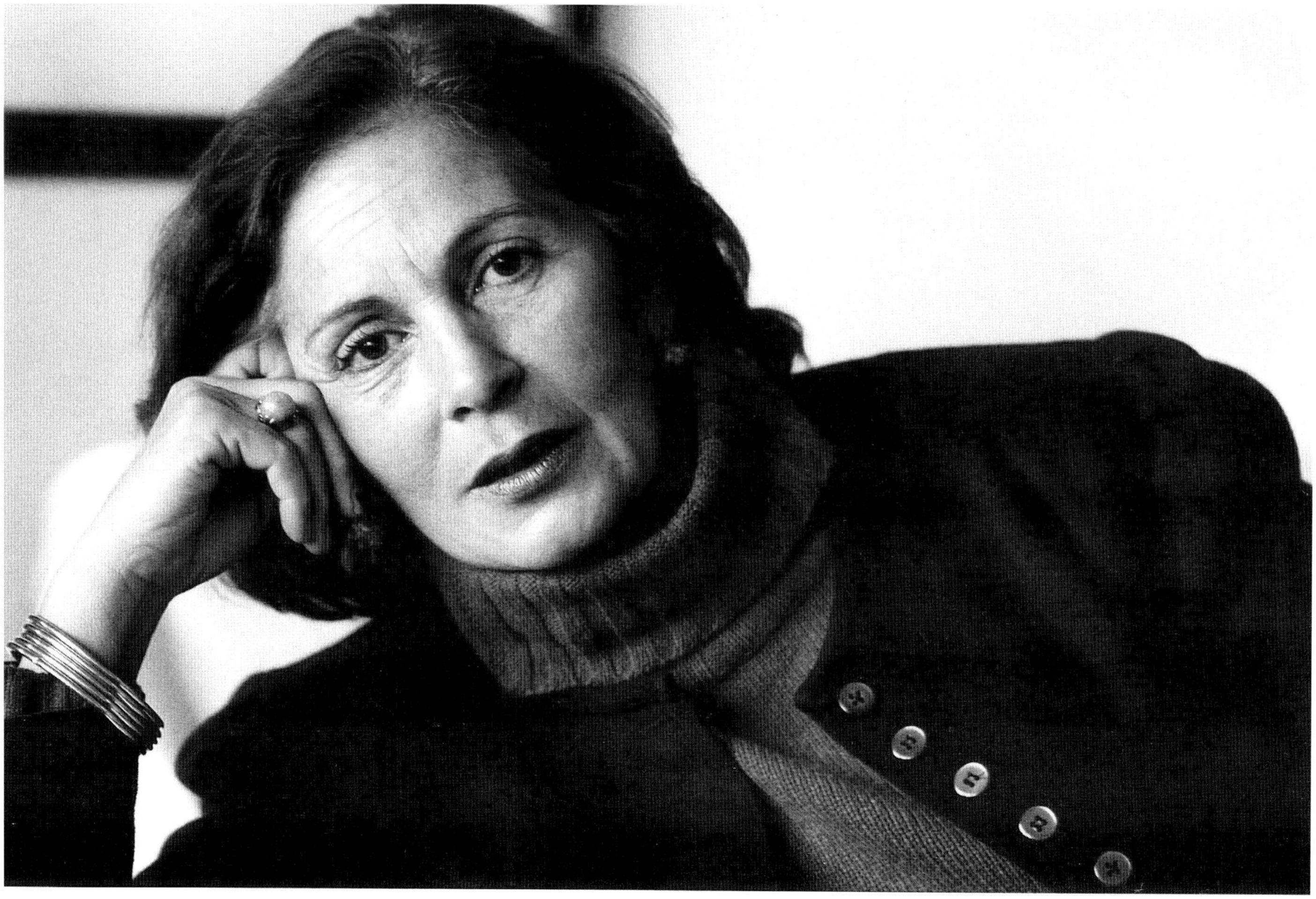

THE TREE BARK

I saw her for the first time, from the back, on the TV.

The journalist wanted to present this woman who had been selected to represent France as an artist in a major world event, but she did not want or could not look at the camera. I immediately thought of the "mal-être" of this woman. "My God, how much pain... she needs help!".

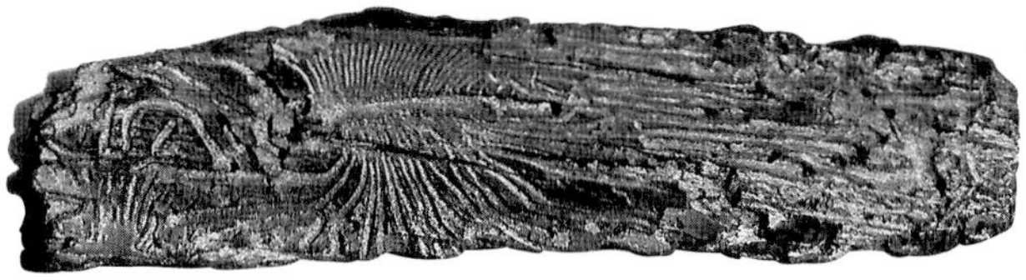

Two weeks later, miracle or chance, she was in my office. It has been one of the most important meetings I ever had as a doctor. Her psychotherapy was exceptionally intense and short. Everything was magical with this woman who had been humiliated by life, hated by her mother and whose survival could only be accomplished through the grace of her creative talent: twigs, leaves and stones, gathered in nature, became works of art in her hands and these re-creations enabled her to escape a much too sordid reality.

The work we did has been as extraordinary as her past. This patient struck me because I never heard about a darker childhood than hers, and I never experienced a shorter and most gratifying work.

Usually, months, or years are necessary to learn to love oneself and become self-assured; with her, after twelve meetings, her rebirth became possible. She had accomplished all the survival path, she only missed the appreciative look of an outsider. I was only a permission, an authorization, a ferment without which her final flight towards living would have been compromised.

At the end of her therapy, she gave me a gift: a simple tree bark chiseled by insects and erosion; she had enhanced the surface with silver. I keep it preciously in my office. It gives me the strength I sometimes need for more difficult patients.

This humble piece of bark is a symbol of our meeting; the look of the artist and her painter's gesture have revealed the beauty of the insects work, of nature and of time; likewise I have been the revealer of the contained beauty of this patient.

This present reminds me all the time that suffering cannot be measured and that solutions always come up. Art is in nature for those who know how to look. Small miracles exist: it is clear that this object which is much more than a piece of wood is the proof of it.

Manigé Auriol
Psychiatrist

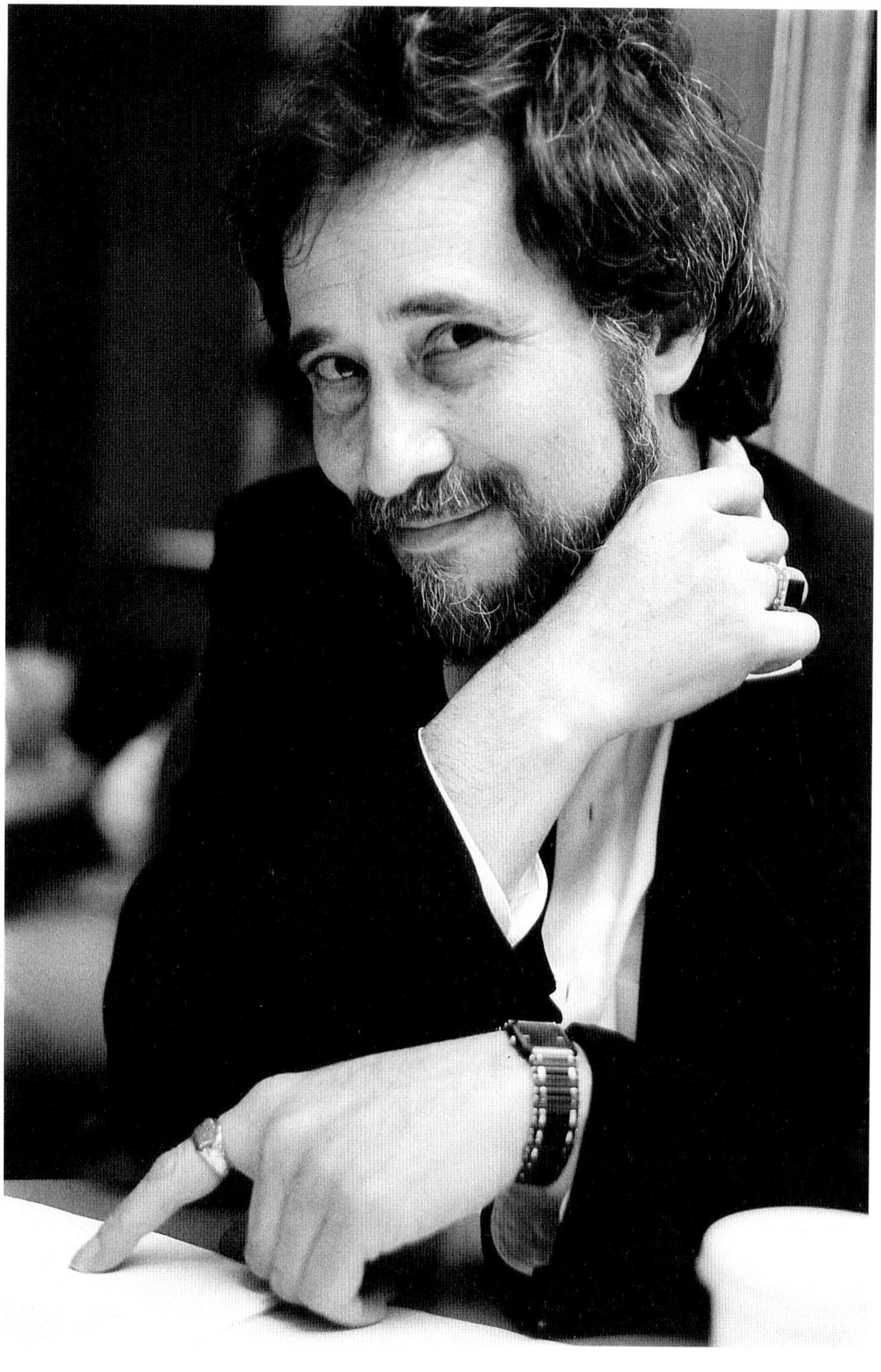

PORTRAIT OF A RING

It is a ring, a thought pressed round to tie the mind, a reminder raised from other ages to bind the present to an unknown past, a memory minted in gold. The past was brought as a present, and it grapples the skin with silk to its touch, with the polished smoothness of wrought metal, with a necessity that will not slip by.

I received it from my grandfather. It is a ring his uncle gave him, for him to pass on, and he gave it to me rather than to his son, for reasons he never told me, for reasons I cannot guess. He came as a boy to the United States from the Ukraine. He came alone, during the Russian Civil War, running ahead of the White Army, who were being chased across the Ukraine by the Red Army conscripting everyone in their path. It took him two years to work his way across Europe and depart for the U.S., to meet this uncle, who later gave him the ring.

I grew up in his house, and in all the years since, he has remained my touchstone for manhood, the person of my past who modeled for me the requirements of a good life, the standards to which we must hold ourselves, the standards we elect to guide us, the demands we could choose to omit but which we are supposed to know better than to dismiss. He set for me the bar by which to measure a life well lived, and he gave his ring to me.

I wear that ring on the forefinger of my left hand. I wear it always, to remind me of something I have yet to understand, something that has come to me from a century gone and half a world away. And now I find as I mature as a writer, those authors who matter most to me, authors of the fantastic and dire imagination, authors of the terrible dream Gogol, Bruno Schulz, Leivick, Nabokov come from cities and villages in that same part of the world, in the part of the world from which part of me has come. Their homes form nearly a ring around the village in which my grandfather was born, the village he fled. And now I sense a destiny is drawing close.

Mark Daniel Cohen
Writer

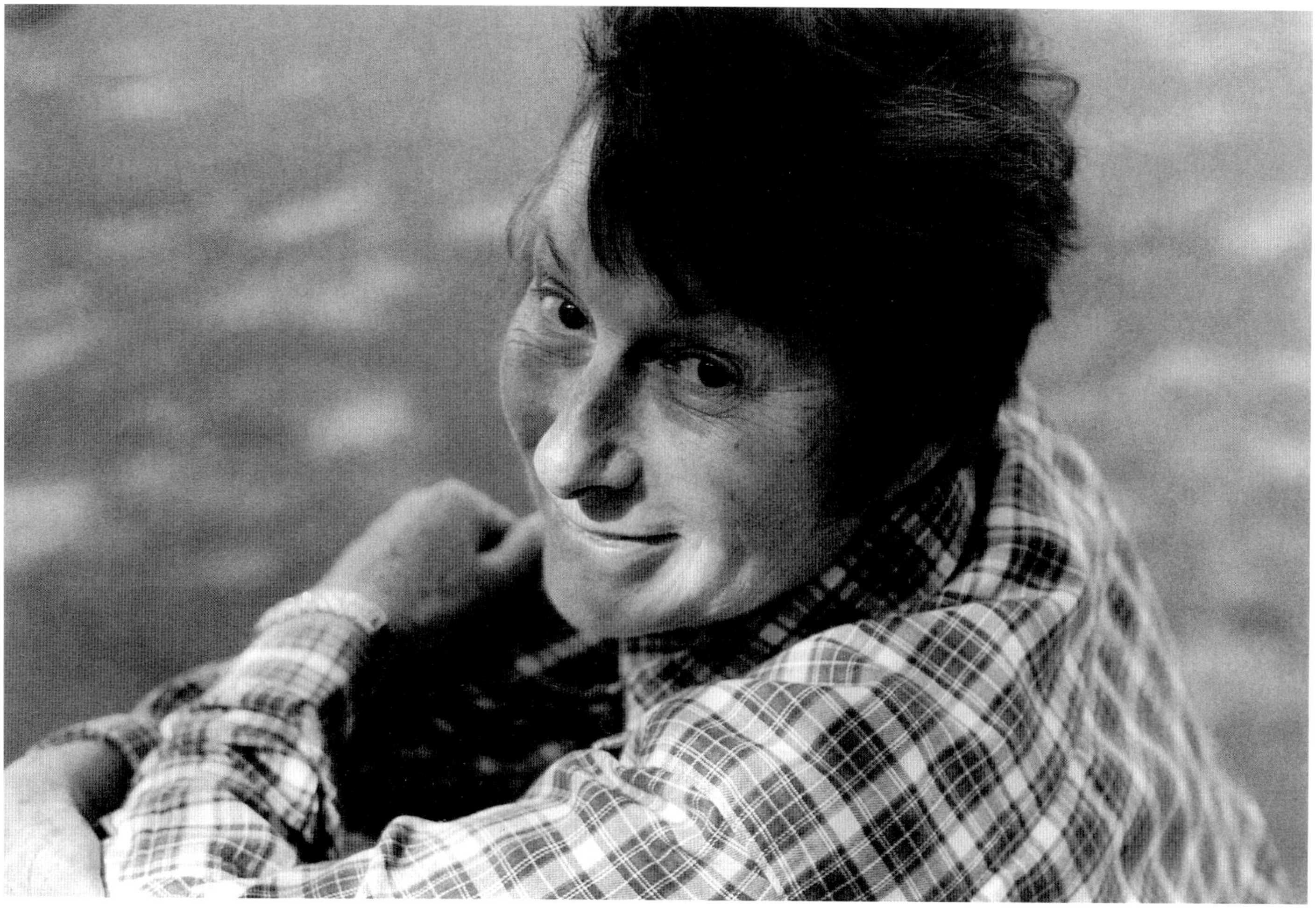

THE CARNELIAN RING

Her hands were those of a worker. Square, not well taken care of, short nails, and she always wore the same ring, made of carnelian and chiseled silver.

A ring, the only one, which embellished and refined her hand, a ring burnished by time and works, a ring which she caressed once in a while. A ring offered to her on a day of happiness.

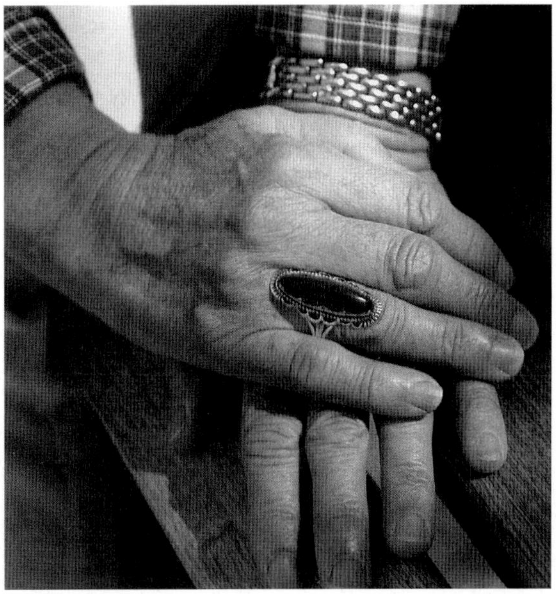

It was during Paris "crazy years", two young people from the province who started in life. For their engagement, he wanted to offer her a "real ring", probably made of white gold and small pieces of diamond, but she refused. As far as she was concerned, she thought of a house and furniture and found that these bourgeois traditions were not appropriate.

Then, on the first occasion, after his first bonus for the first concluded business, he gave her this ring, made of silver and chiseled silver.

And for ever, I saw on her finger this proof of love and fidelity.

Years passed. Her hands became spotted and the story developed as a tale for wise children, and she added, mischievously and sagacious, caressing the carnelian and chiseled silver, that she would have been better off by accepting the diamond ring, because the furniture disappeared in the war turmoil, but the ring itself, however, remained faithfully on her finger, made of carnelian and chiseled silver.

Years passed.

My mother left us slowly, very slowly. And I remember the day when her hand softly caressed mine and put on my finger the ring made of carnelian and chiseled silver, a pledge of love and fidelity.

Dinah Blum
Business Executive

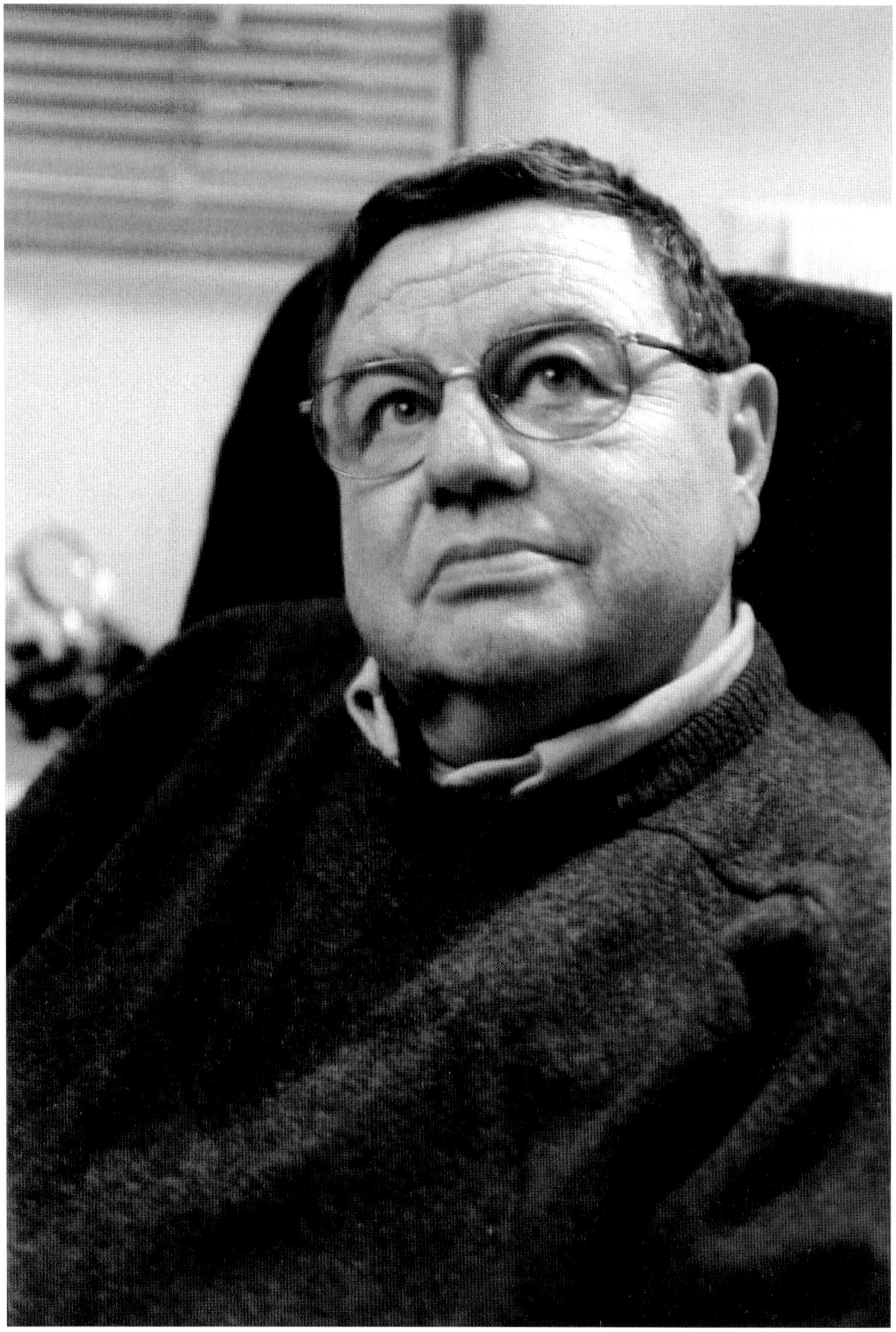

MY SMALL BOAT

Thirty years ago, when I was thirty, my father asked me if I wanted to get back my small boat. He then handed me a small object made of tin; both were dusty because it happened while he was moving out.

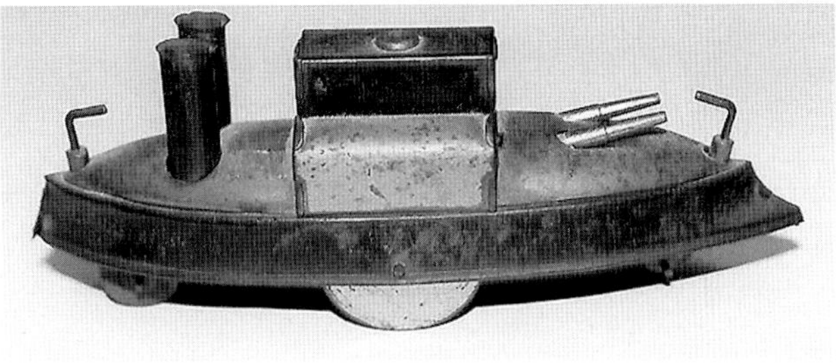

In the back of a raised glass cabinet, a small boat had been put away, out of reach from the hands of a curious, handy but not very careful child.

It was a toy on wheels, from the beginning of the last century, only a few centimeters high, and it was a coarse reproduction of one of those cruisers used before the 1914 war.

Like the big ones it had lost its mast and even its flag. Its large and small wheels had been object of a rough repair in the nineteen fifties with two tin wheels cut out of a tin box and put together with the heads of thumbtacks. After this repair, my father had carefully decided to put away this object "so that I could enjoy it later".

This story happened years ago, when I turned four, during my first visit to my grandparents, in a small village of Normandy which had just been liberated. It was the time when a child was introduced to the Society.

Near the village was a "castle", a large XVIIth century mansion with a park, where a respectable family lived. After the presentation, and so that the adults could carry on their conversation, I was kept busy with a "toy", remembrance of times past. But, upon our leaving, the fight was tough. There was no giving up on my part; I kept the object, to my grandparents' shame.

This is the small boat which I preciously kept and which I plan to give to a special restorer who will give back to the boat the honor due to it.

My grandparents passed away, the generous "donors" also and so no one can claim it. It is mine to keep.

Henri Courtois
Human Resources Manager

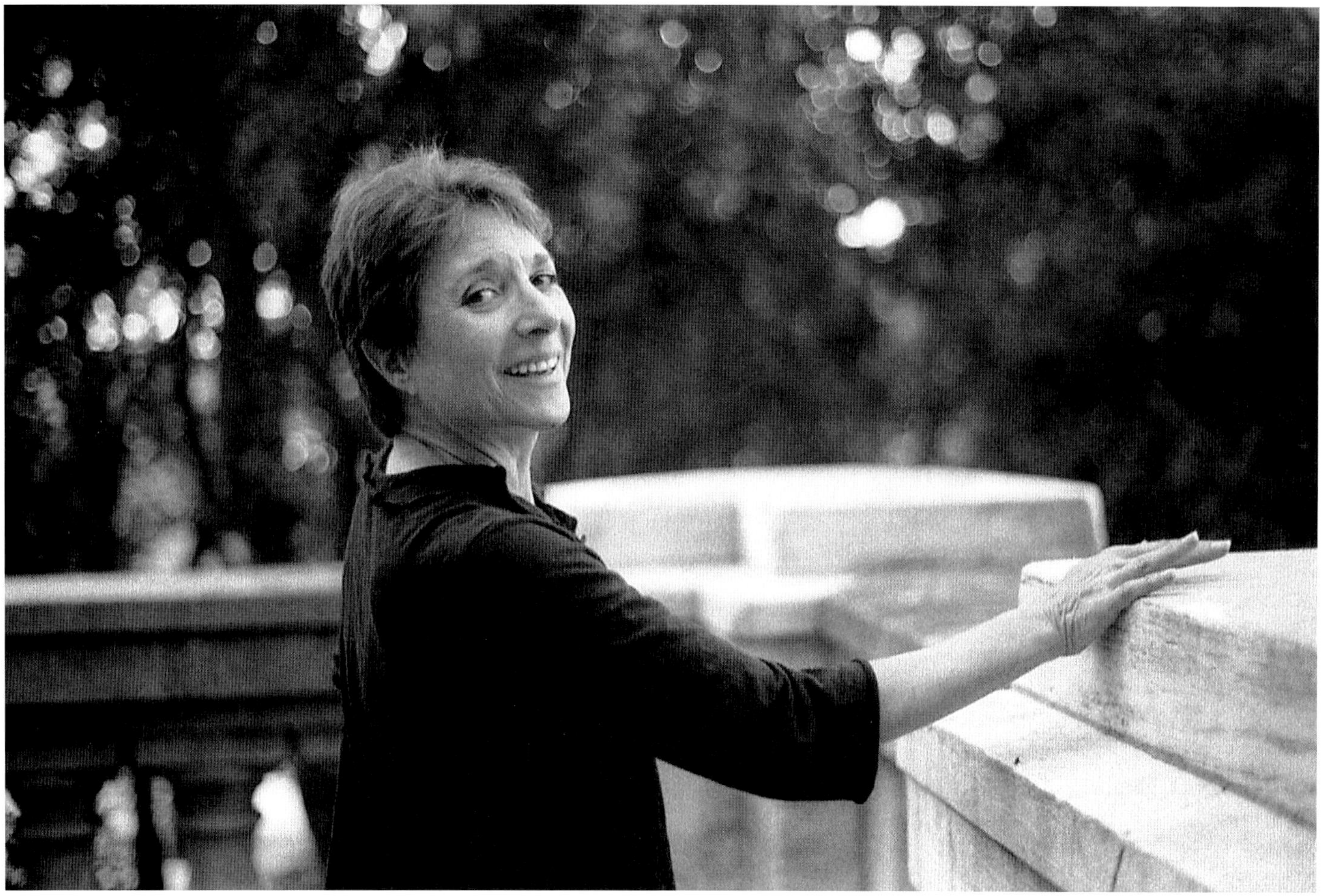

THE SILVER WATCH

I never thought things would mean much to me. I never had a jewelry collection or many things surrounding me in my home. But, I have discovered that special objects can inspire recollections and allow a return to the past.

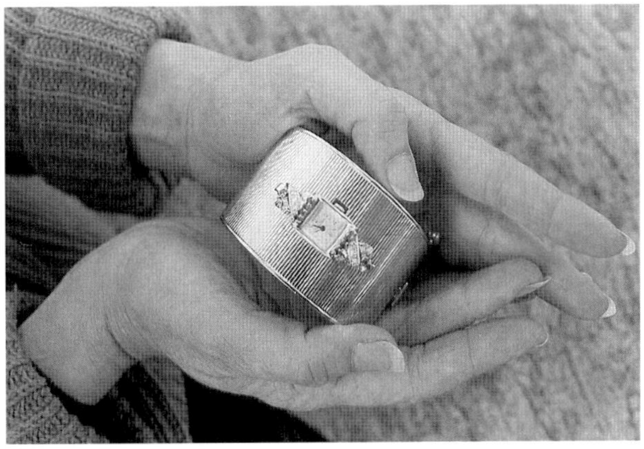

As a little girl, living in Queens, life was relatively simple and filled with routines. On Saturday nights, my very beautiful and elegant parents would go out for the evening. This always required my father's napping after a golf game and my mother's primping and dressing in a softly lighted and mirrored dressing room.

It was in this room that I would very carefully watch my mother's perfected routine; first the underwear and then the combing and styling of her hair. This was followed by a slow application of colorful cheeks, carefully applied lip liner, softly penciled eyebrows and firmly applied lipstick. Nothing however compared to her indelicate spitting into her dried mascara and harshly ribbing a small brush back and forth. With eyes wide, she would slowly and carefully apply the black and pasty covering to her eyelashes – each lash parallel and at attention. Next would be perfume behind each ear, to be followed by high heeled shoes and a dress. For the finale, she adorned herself with jewelry. My most beautiful mother was ready for her evening of fun.

As I write this, my breathing has become much deeper as I relive this simple memory of the love and admiration of a daughter for her mother. Recently, my mother gave me her silver watch and it made me realize that I had unconsciously associated this piece of jewelry with my mother's elegance and beauty. It made me proud to be worthy of this gift from such a magnificent woman.

Judy Graff
Dancer

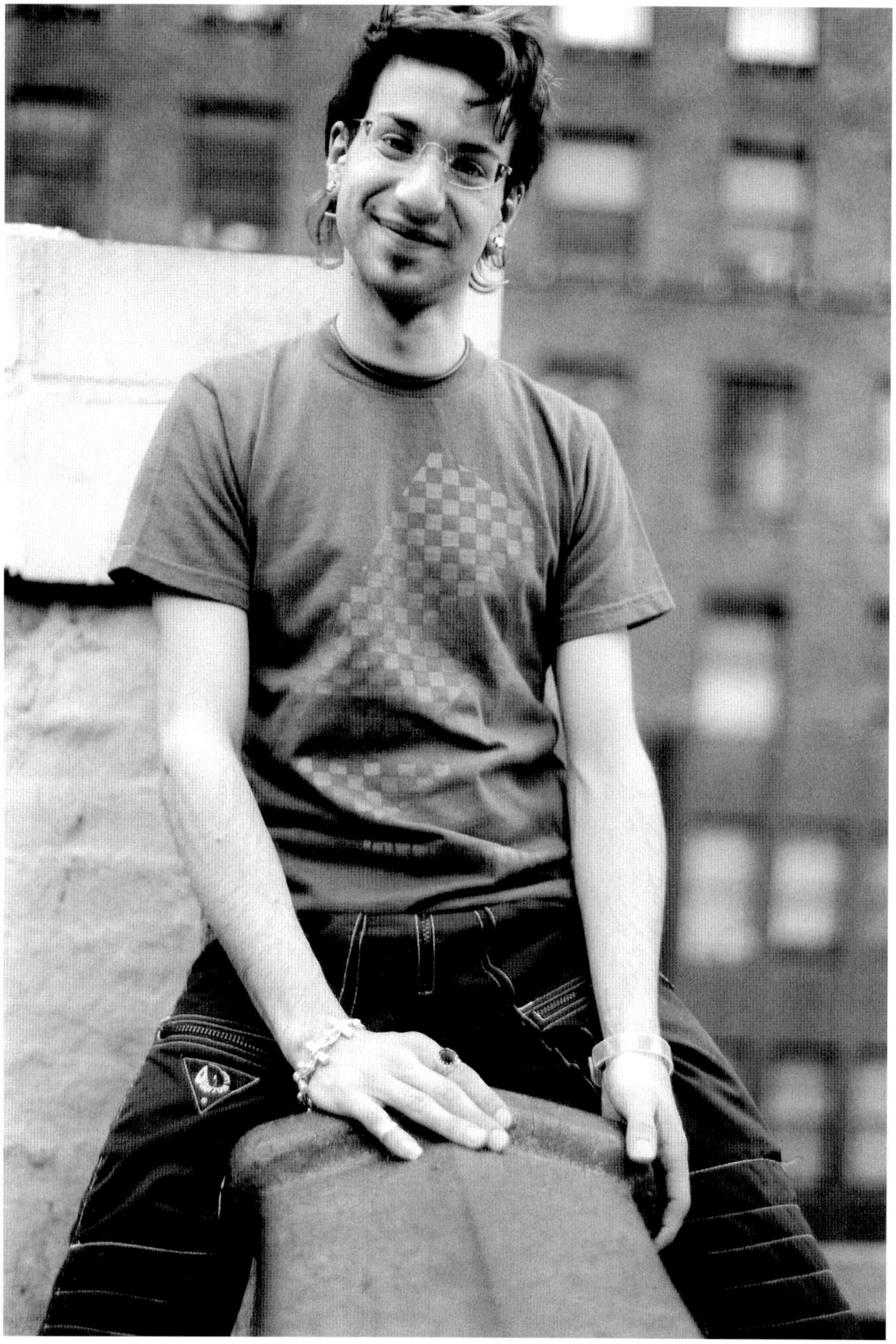

MY FATHER'S RING

There are all sorts of people that come into our lives.

Some people come into our life for just a short period of time, others for a longer period, and others who are in our life forever. Each person is in our life for a reason, to teach or show us something.

When I was asked to be photographed with my favorite object, a few things came to mind; being photographed with my partner, who I deeply care for, being photographed with a tree in a forest because I love all that is growing.

Then I thought of my father, to whom this ring belonged. My father died when I was 19 years old. He was more than just papa, he was my best friend and a teacher of life.

There were three rings, one for each of his sons. When this ring was given to me by my mother, I marveled at it, looking at all the cuts and facets in it and how it reflected light. I wore it only to the funeral. Putting it away, till now. I have begun to feel a connection with it at this point in my life. Although it has been 11 years without my father, I still am learning from him. The one thing that I miss tremendously in my life every day is he, but yet sometimes I can feel him. Now being a man, myself I can appreciate how he lived and the virtues in life. I find myself modeling my life after his, building my morals as he did.

When I wear this ring, it seems to make more sense to me. Sparkling about, I think of him.

Marco Guglielmino
Hairdresser

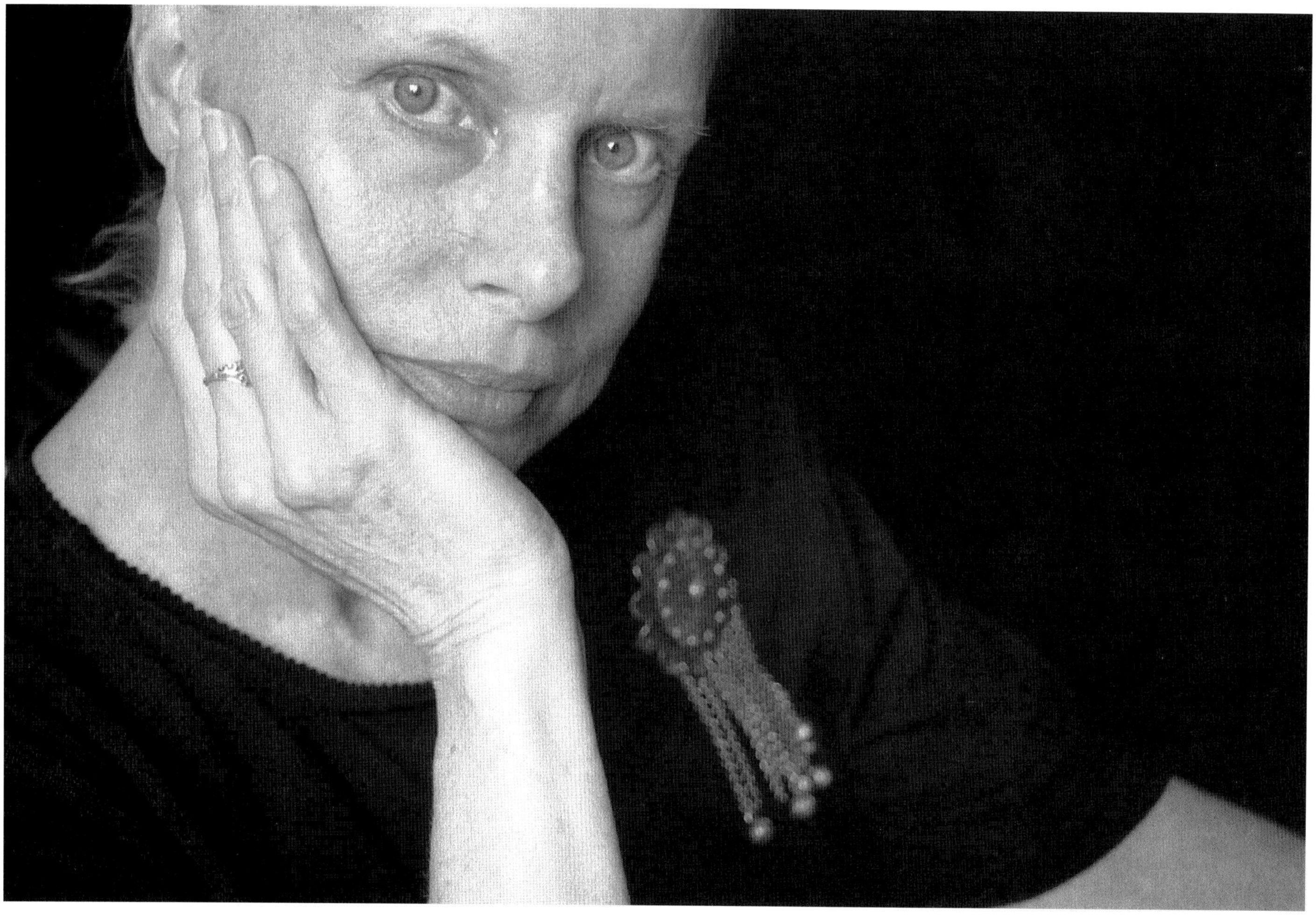

MY GRANDMOTHER'S BROOCH

When Grandma died I received some heirlooms, some rings, bracelets and pins. Most of these were stolen from me during a trip to Europe. I still have this brooch and cherish it. I hold it in my hands and it feels as though my grandmother is still here. I loved my grandma so much. When I was a small child she frequently held me in her arms to lull me to sleep, and she often wore this brooch. I liked to reach up and touch it.

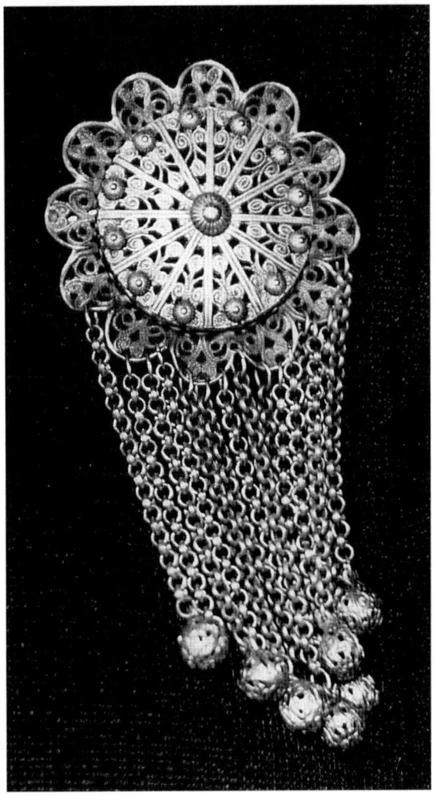

The little hanging chains fascinated me and were fun to play with. I would dangle the chains in my fingers and play until I fell asleep, content. In a way she and I always will be together. I wear her brooch now and vividly remember the grandmother I hold in my heart forever.

Deborah Black
Painter

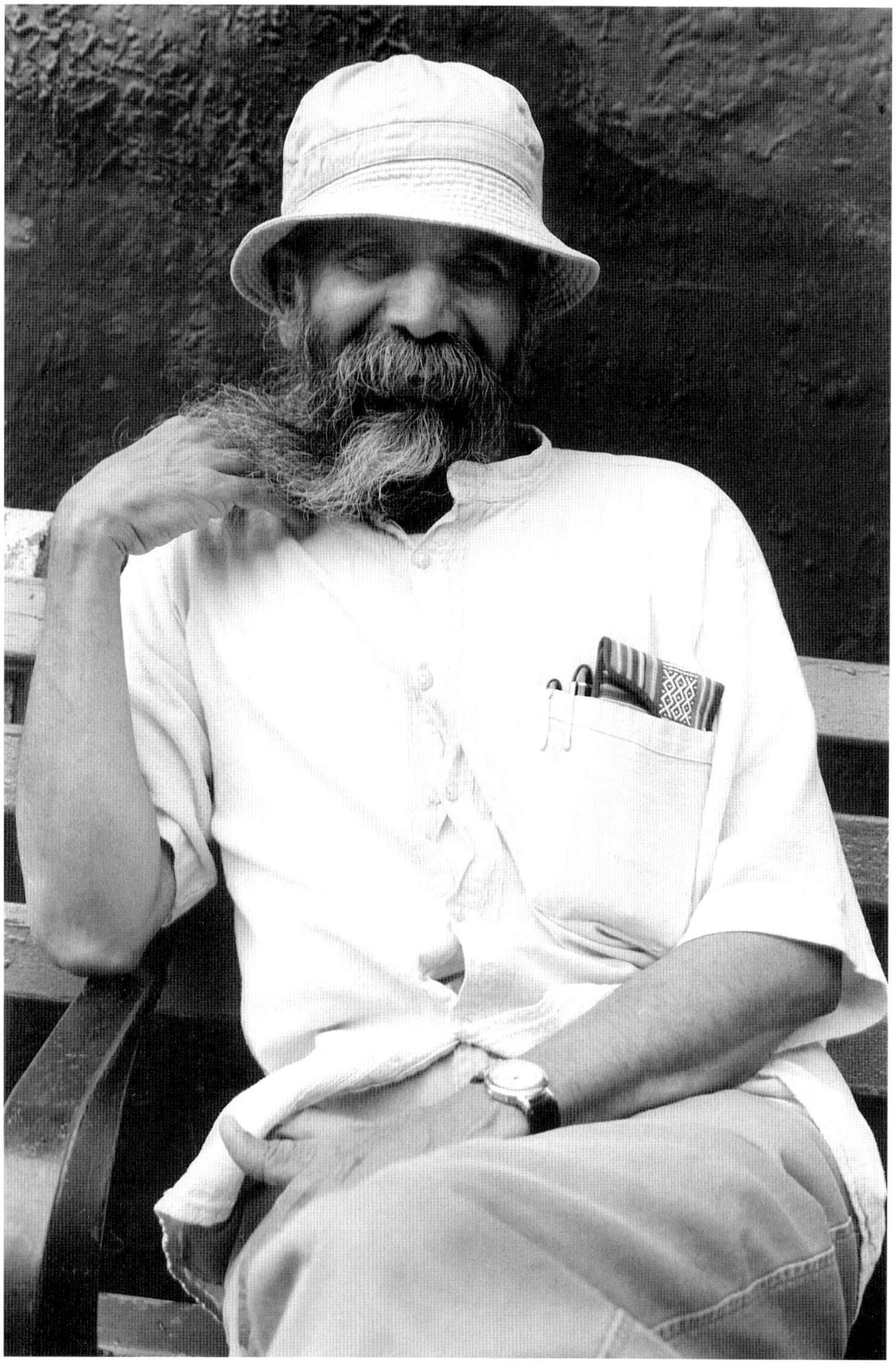

MY PENS

The most significant objects in my life are my pens.

A pen is made to write but for an artist like myself, it is made to draw lines, which is creating life. A writer creates with words, I create with lines.

I started to use an ordinary plastic fountain pen when I was in second grade in India. Later when I was in Madras I purchased a new fountain pen made of ebony. I never liked ball point pens because I found it hard to write and draw with them. During my college years I always used a pen which was refillable with ink and which always leaked in some way. My hands were often dirty because of it.

Now, when I draw, I always use one of my two German pens, as ink leaves a more permanent mark than a pencil.

When I first came to the US, I saw a Montblanc Diplomat pen with an extra broad pen which is what I like when I draw; however it was too expensive. Several years later it was still expensive, but I was able to purchase one at a better price and I also realized that by selling just one work I could pay for it. So I bought it and always carry it with me to this day.

My other pen is a Pelikan with an extra fine point, which I originally purchased for my older son when I sent him back to India. A couple of years later during a visit with him, I saw the pen lying unused around the house. He told me he had no use for it, so I took it back. These two pens, or at least one of them, are always in my shirt pocket and I draw with both of them. One has a fine point and the other one an extra large point and they are used accordingly.

These two pens are with me all the time as a part of my clothing, and they travel with me everywhere.

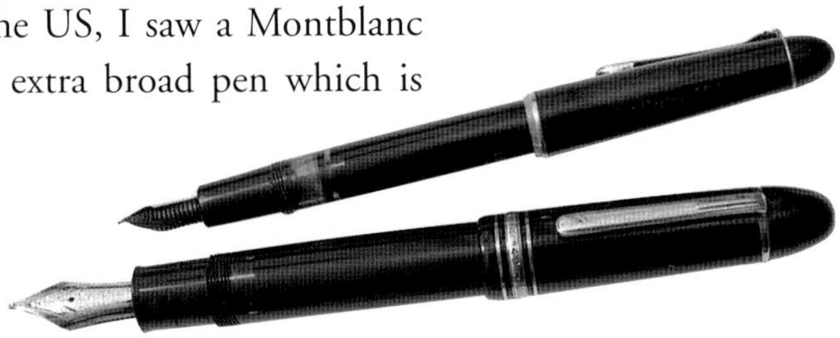

Sumatimohan Van
Painter

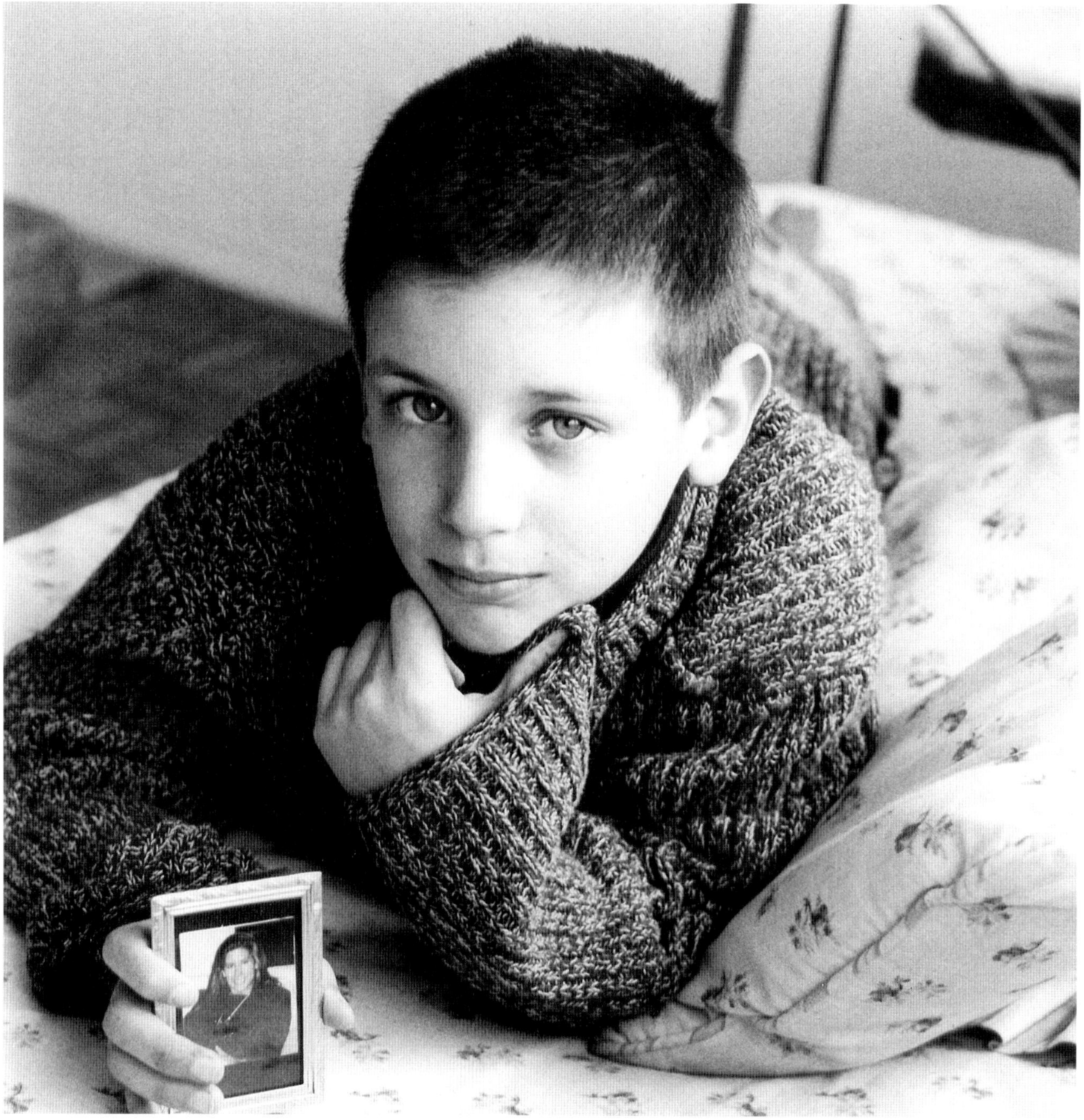

MY MOM'S PICTURE

I have a book *The Cat in the Hat* by Dr. Seuss which I read at least twenty times and which I like so much, but my preferred object is this special picture of my Mom which I have kept since I was 6 years old. I was told that it was taken when I was two. It is small and I always had it in a frame.

Before I moved to New York, I kept it near the computer in the kitchen, but now it stays in my bedroom. That way I can always see her face if she is not around; it's a bit like having a double Mommy. I think she looks happy in that picture and that she is very beautiful. I never took it with me when I was going away some place, though, because I have always been afraid to lose it.

Christopher Cimperman
Highschool Student

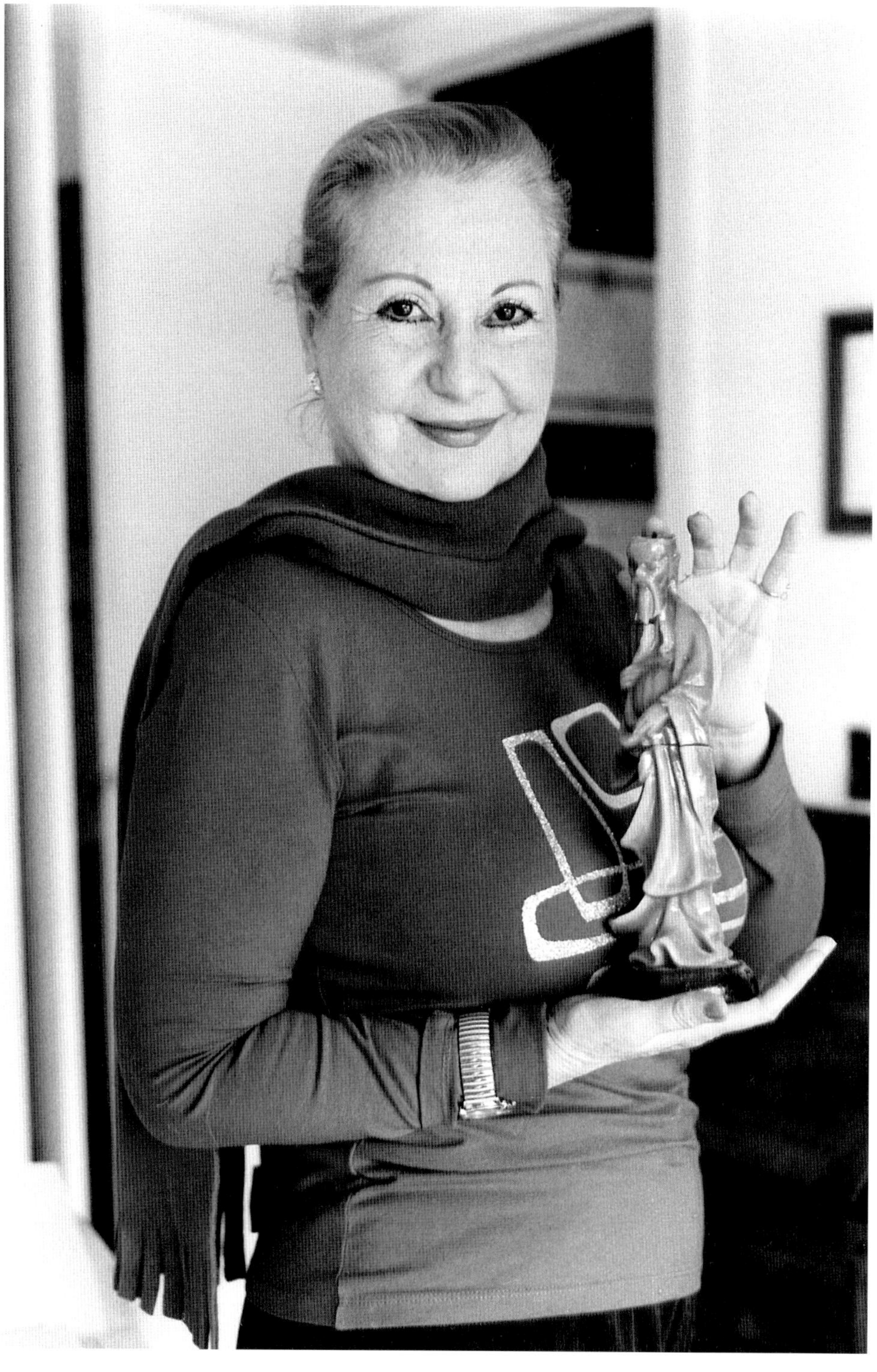

THE SAFFRON CANDLE

One day, when I was nine years old, I saw in the window of a Rue d'Antibes shop, in Cannes, a saffron colored candle in the shape of an old "wise man" draped in a long robe. It looked elegant just like the ancient Chinese sculptures.

This little man fascinated me. It told me of listening, appeasing goodness and protection. All these things I would have liked to find in my father who did not always understood my motivations. The idea to offer it to him as a present for the next Christmas came to my mind and I hoped to be able to save enough money until I could purchase it.

I went to the store where I explained my project to the saleswoman, and she promised to put it aside for me. Every week I would check if my little statue was still in the window of this nice store, believing that it would tempt many passers-by.

I ended up being able to offer it to my father, who put it on a shelf where it seemed to be protecting my whole family.

Twenty years later, I met a man. He looked just like my statue.
He was just as wise.

When I was nine years old, I had perceived that such a person did exist in real life.
Half a century has passed and the statue is still with me and so is the man who looks so much like it.

Nicole Lemaire d'Agaggio
Painter
General Secretary of French Academy of Sciences, Arts and Letters

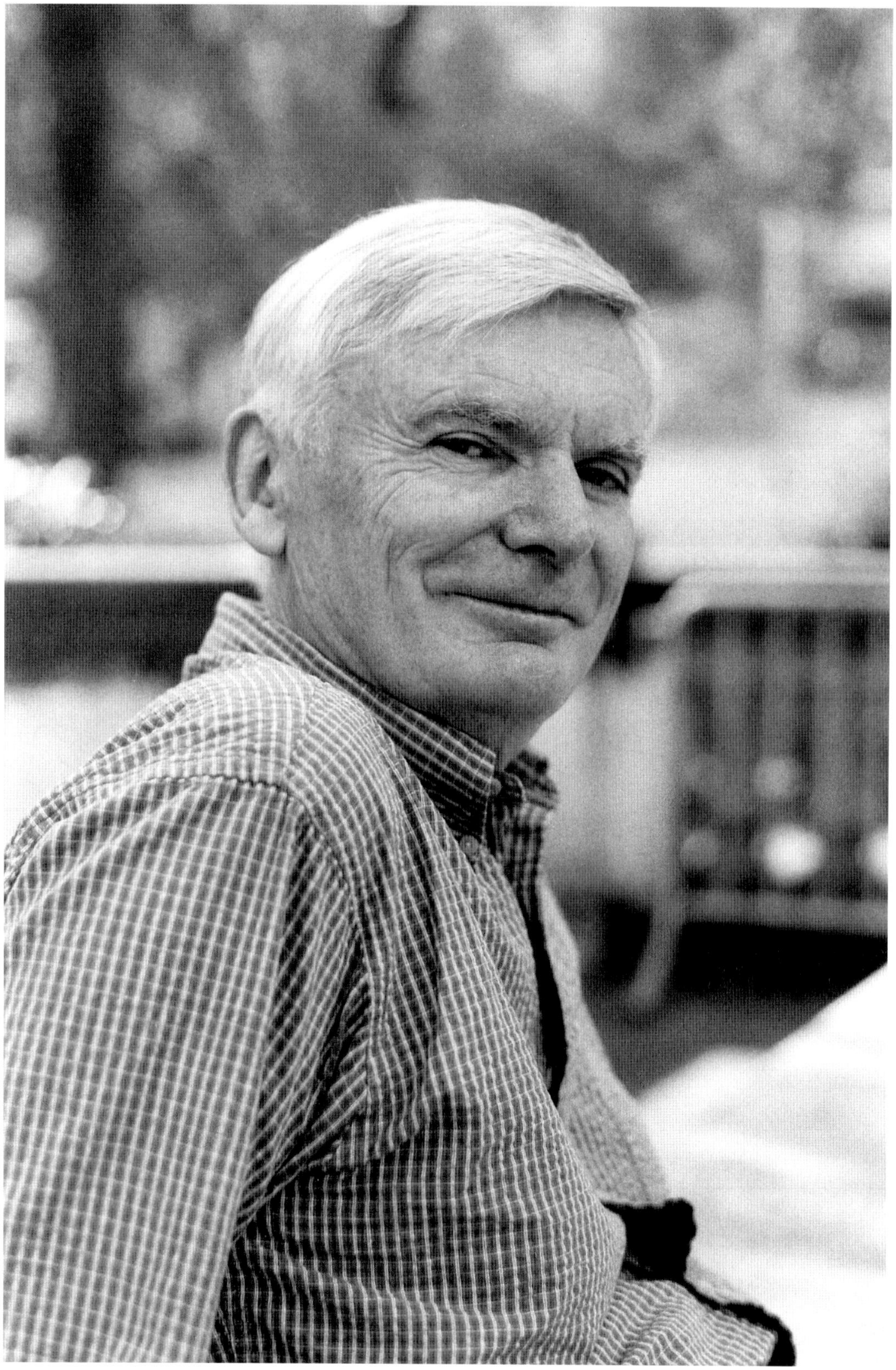

THE LITTLE AXE IN POLISHED STONE

It was summer, more than forty years ago. I often jogged with a friend on a dirt road which follows a brook and passes a sort of dull blue-green water hole almost completely covered with leaves.

This friend, a student like myself, believed Algeria was a part of France. As General de Gaulle was bringing the Algerian war to an end, my friend got mixed up in a failed plot to assassinate de Gaulle. When the police were about to catch him, he hurriedly passed me a revolver.

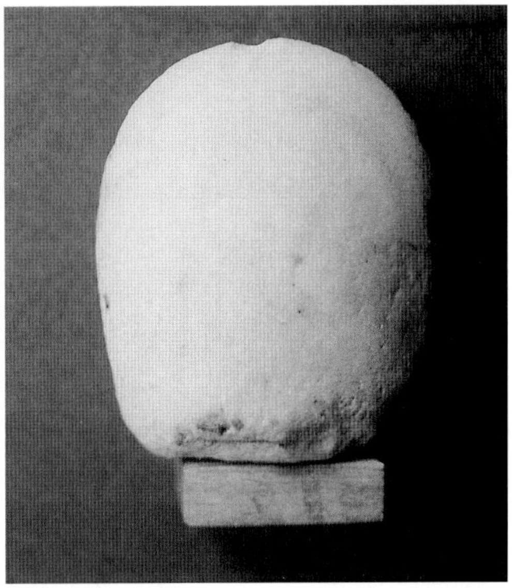

Suddenly I had to choose between friendship and my own convictions, and so I went jogging and threw this poisoned gift in the water hole.

Some days later, jogging along the same road, a shiny stone buried in the soil caught my attention. The pure curve of its polished edge led me to understand that it was a Neolithic axe. I like to think of this find as a reward for saving my friend. I have it framed with a short text explaining that this axe probably dates back to two or three thousand years B.C. and was certainly used in the clearing of the forest of the Parisian basin.

Claude Dassule
Engineer

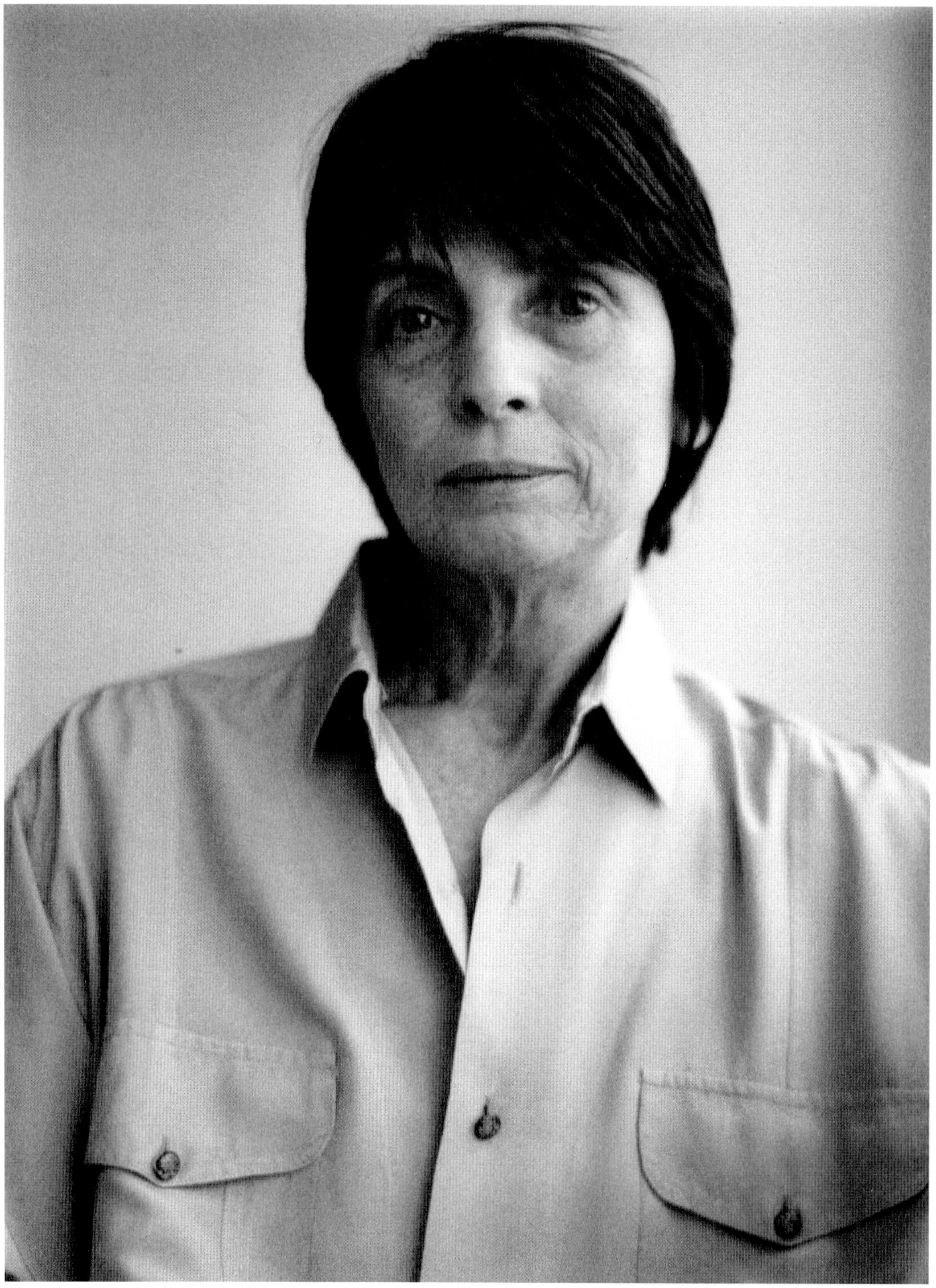

THE WATCH

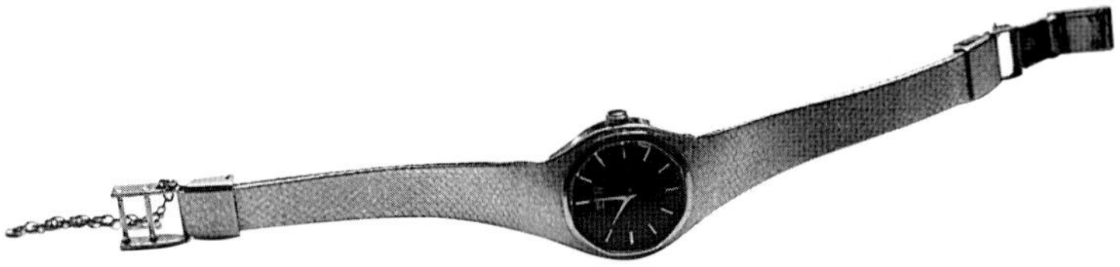

It is winter, the crossroads of Belleville and Pyrénées, the street descends and then the park. At times I loved to walk, to look at the opened shutters on the third floor, to count the windows, the lounge, the kitchen, the rooms. Yes, it was late in the evening, close to the fireplace, the blue drawn curtains, he said that he wished to show me something in the little brown box. A watch. A jewel as impenetrable as it was beautiful. The disegno of the bracelet, with its particular neatness, its very smooth and cold curve. It gives itself to the gaze in its isolated nakedness, suspended in the roundness of a silky cavity. The memory is very precise, the bare movement of my hand closing the box. For a long time I have thought that in this gesture there was a fleeing from touch, from corporal contact.

This watch, I refused to wear it. There was something searing in this refusal.

It is winter; the little brown box is definitely lost. The watch was also forgotten. That day the watch has turned up, the exterior envelope is open, a profound wound in the flesh exposing the entrails. I have remained stricken by the image, by the strangeness of the organic depth. I felt the capture of my gaze within the opening as far as touching death.

Blanca Lloret
Artist

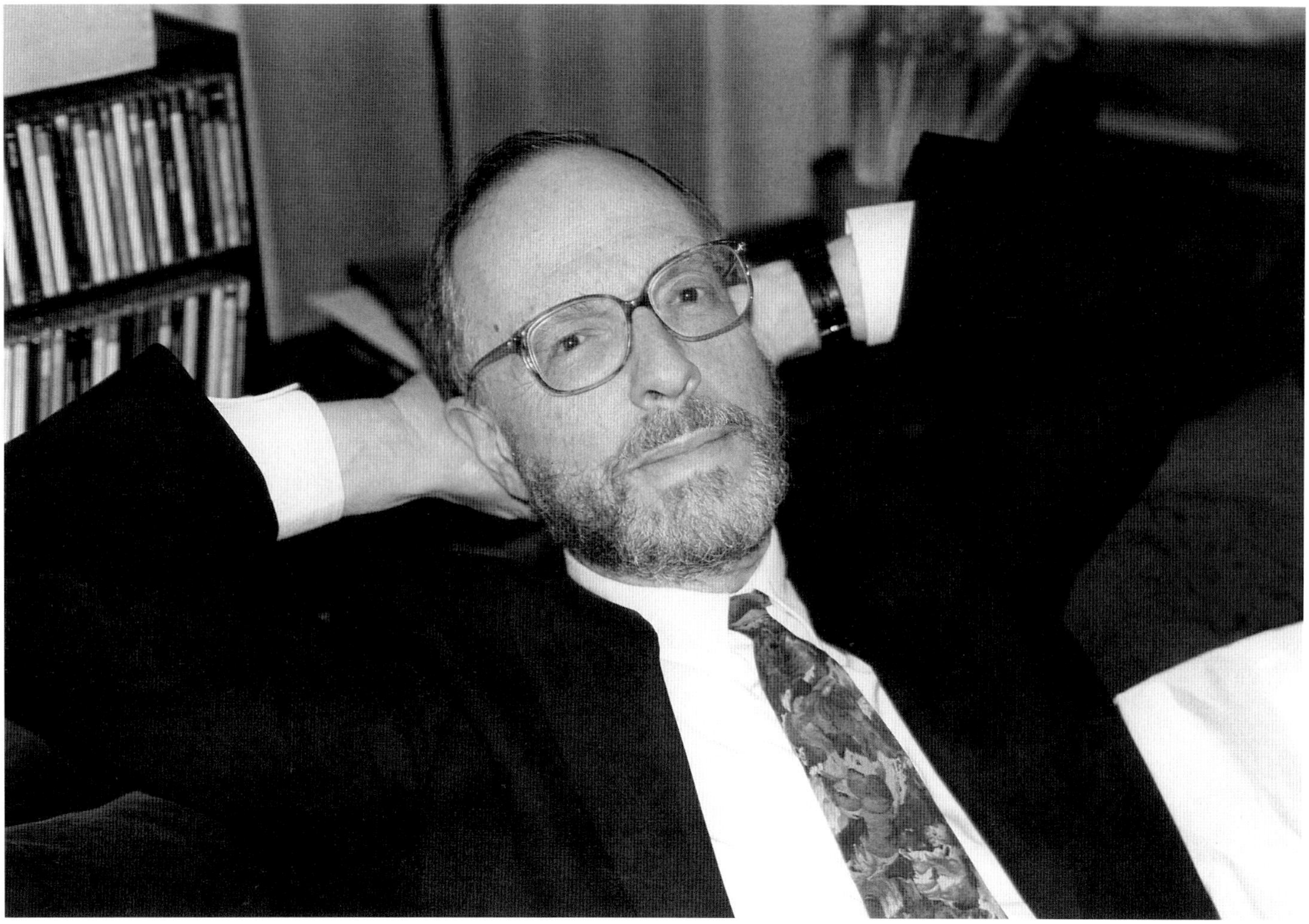

THE PASSPORT PHOTOS

My parents came from a part of the world that changed profoundly and frequently over the last century and a bit. Although the coordinates were almost the same, the countries and even the civilizations were different. When my father was born there in 1897, it was Austria-Hungary. He spoke German and that was the predominant culture. He remembered how they had to swear allegiance to Kaiser Karl when Franz Josef died and he told me opera bouffe tales of the Austrian army on the Russian front. When my mother was born there in 1913, it was about to become Poland and those who spoke German but not Polish, like my father, were not welcome. She spoke of the wonderful universities and the culture of Paderewski and what wonderful Polish her mother spoke. After the Second World War, the region became part of the USSR and now it's in the Ukraine. No one speaks German or Polish there anymore.

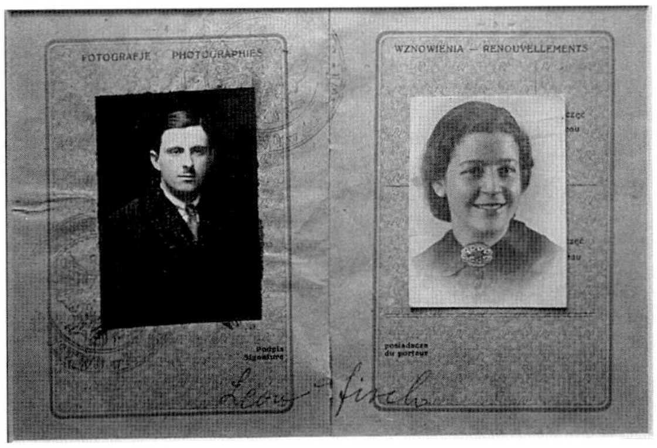

In my father's passport photo from 1925, he has something of the Austro-Hungarian look, with the Astrakhan coat and the little moustache. In my mother's photo from 1937, she's very fresh and pretty but her style has a Slavic charm. Since she knew Polish but not German, the fact they were married at all was a tribute to his determination and her willingness to take risks. In 1936, my father went from Indianapolis to meet my mother, then 23, based on a photograph and a brief correspondence in extremely broken Polish. Four days later they were married and he returned to America while she unsuccessfully tried to obtain a visa until finally my father's congressman intervened and paved the way. Each of them lived in a vibrant, colorful European world that is completely gone just as they are gone. My last contacts are these two photos and the many stories I heard over the years. Yet the pictures show that perhaps not all the stories were totally accurate. My mother always hated any kind of facial hair and it was only when I obtained the photos that I learned my father used to have a moustache. When my mother died, I grew a beard.

Michael Fisch
VP of Research of main Chemical Company

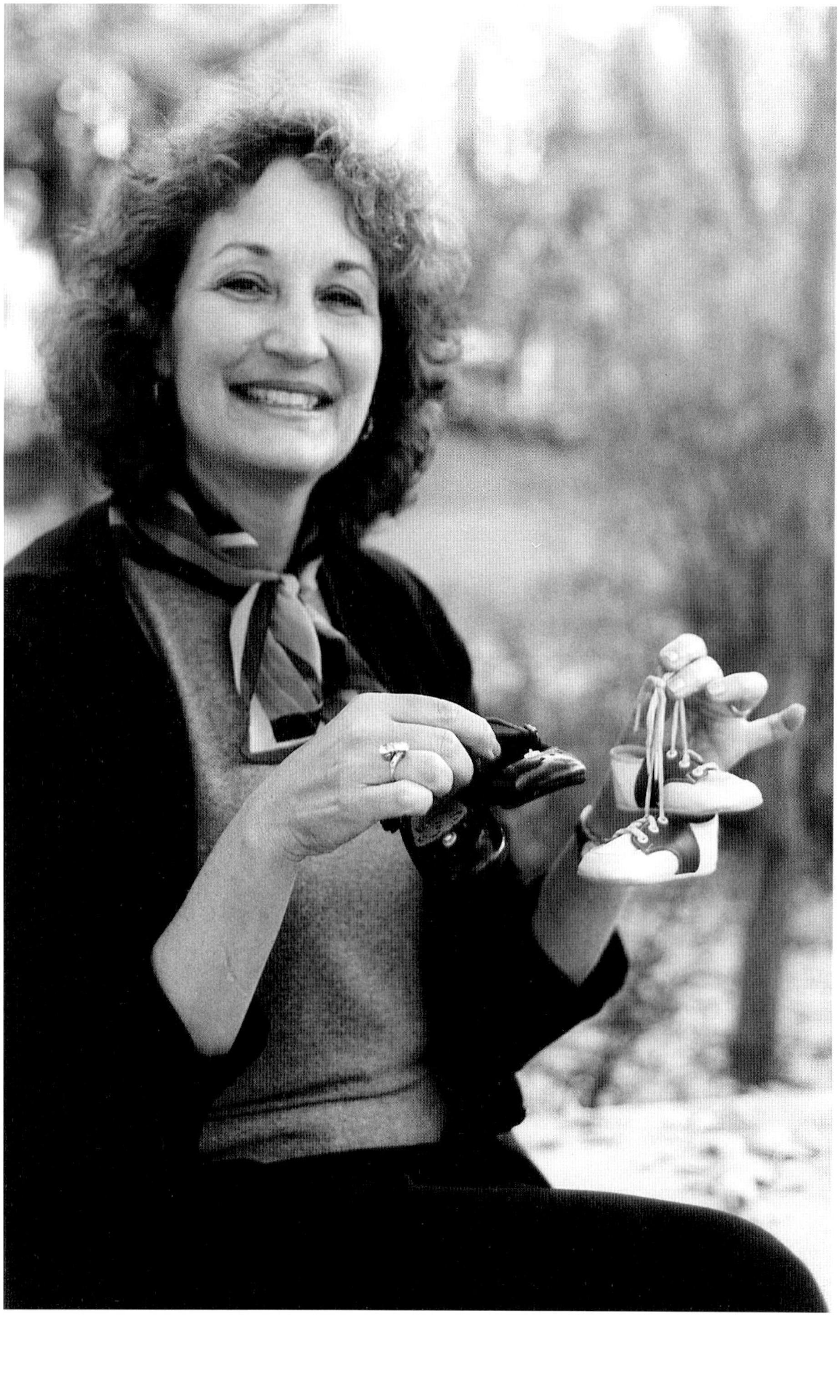

MY PENDANT

I love jewels which have a story.

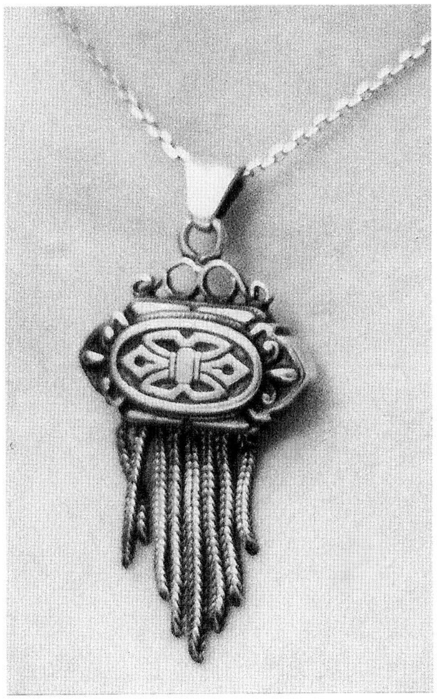

In my family, for instance, in the past four generations, a ring goes from mother to daughter. It is offered to the young woman when she "enters life". It changes with generations; it is for her introduction to the world or when she turns 21, or when she starts going to the university. Presently this piece of jewelry is in the hand of my daughter, until the next generation.

The pendant story is more recent. In the eighties-nineties, my husband Henri and I went to an antique dealer in the Lot area. Henri wanted to give me a gift and he asked the dealer what kind of antique jewelry he had. The man had very little, but I discovered a small silver object from the beginning of the last century that Henri gave me.

In reality, it was a man's watch fob. I can well visualize it on the chain of a notary public, or a country doctor or coming out of the pocket of a well-fed cattle merchant wearing his fancy clothes.

After getting familiarized with this object, touching it, feeling it, I decided to make a pendant out of it. I discussed with the antique dealer and chose a large flat ring. I "diverted" this object by transforming it from a man's piece of jewelry into a woman's pendant.

Every time I wear this pendant, it reminds me a little bit of the history of a French province, the Lot, which my husband was able to adopt. Also, by the "transformation" of this piece of jewelry, I feel that I changed its destiny and was part of a creative process.

Bernadette Courtois
Adults Training Consultant

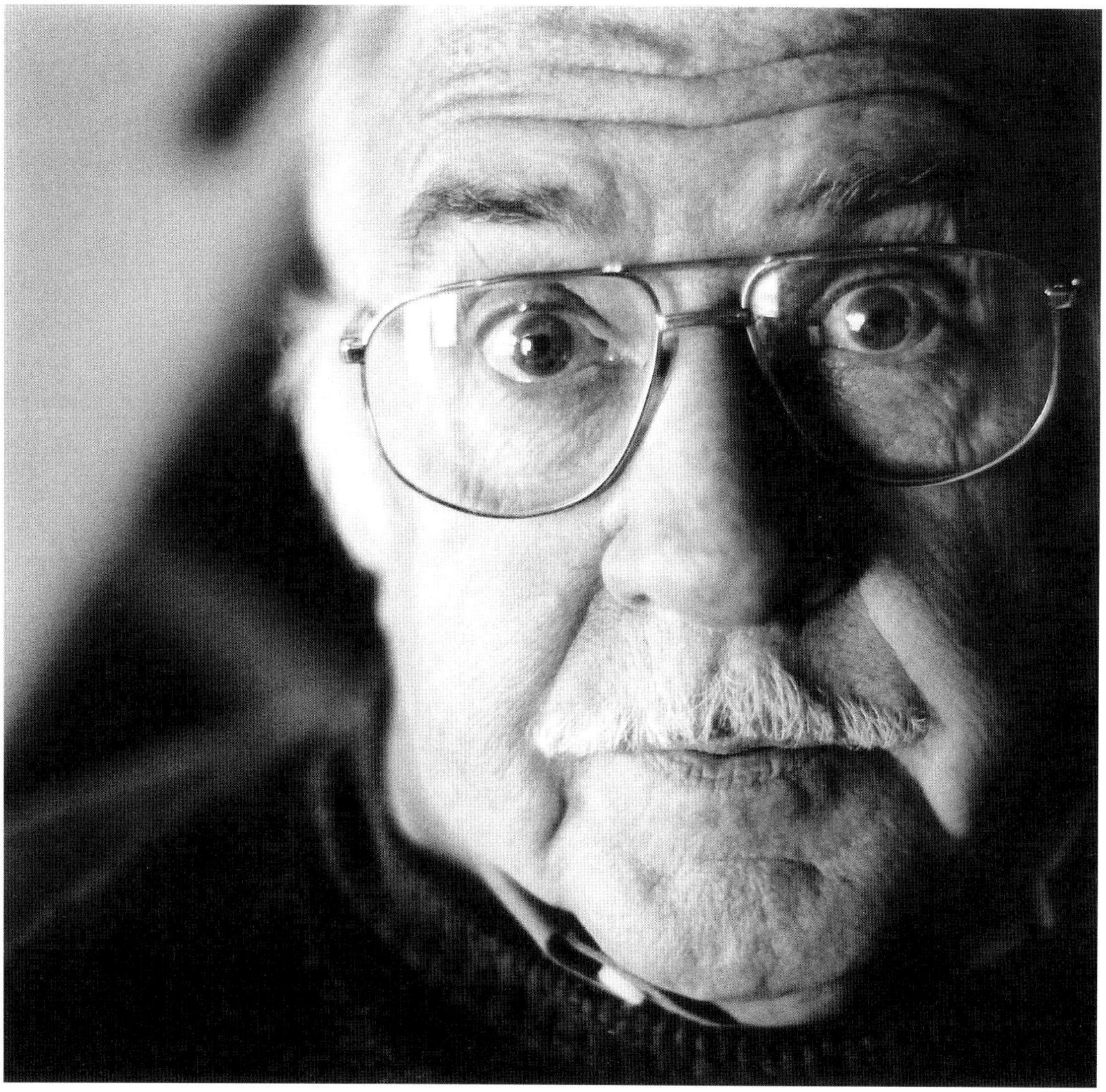

BEYOND THE WHITE PAGE

When I was about eight years old, I would spend hours drawing, particularly on Thursdays when there was no school. It was a guilty delight since I found it so pleasurable. "Instead of spending time drawing, you should be working on your maths ", my mother would yell. One thing is certain, the family did not encourage the birth of a vocation, of which I myself was not much aware then. I never had any hope of extracting from them a few cents to buy drawing paper. For me, a white page was not a page, it was a miracle.

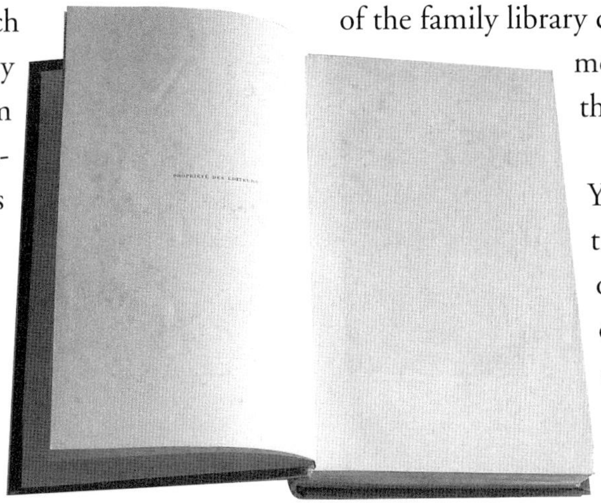

The first books that fell victims to my voraciousness for white paper were the four volumes of the Quillet Encyclopedia. I carefully cut out the fly-pages. It was beautiful heavy satin-like paper, slightly ivory colored. Then there were all the fly-pages of books with gold and red bindings, books that I had been given as school prizes. "Bouffant" paper with a light grain. Among the many titles, I remember Walter Scott's *Quentin Durward*, Théophile Gautier's *Capitaine Fracasse*, Alfred de Vigny's *Fifth of March* and *Servitude et Grandeur Militaire*. All of them in folio size upon which I would draw with a lead pencil. I also remember drawing in ink on the fly-pages of a very handsome edition of *Récit d'une Expédition au Spitzberg*, with woodcuts of terrifying scenes. Pierre Mac Orlan's *Anchor of Compassion* suffered the same fate. When the resources of the family library dried up, I very naturally, and most innocently, used those of the Public Library.

Years passed. I became an illustrator and graphic designer and often had the opportunity to do layouts for books; expensive ones or paperbacks. I always made sure that the fly-page, or page one, as well as the last page -- which, in French books, is often on the backside of the "Achevé d'imprimer"-- were left blank . Today, though the idea is not fully intentional, I like to imagine that, somewhere, a young, intrepid scribbler may have gotten hold of these white pages to refashion the world according to his dreams, in-quartos or in-octavos.

Jean Toche
Graphic Designer

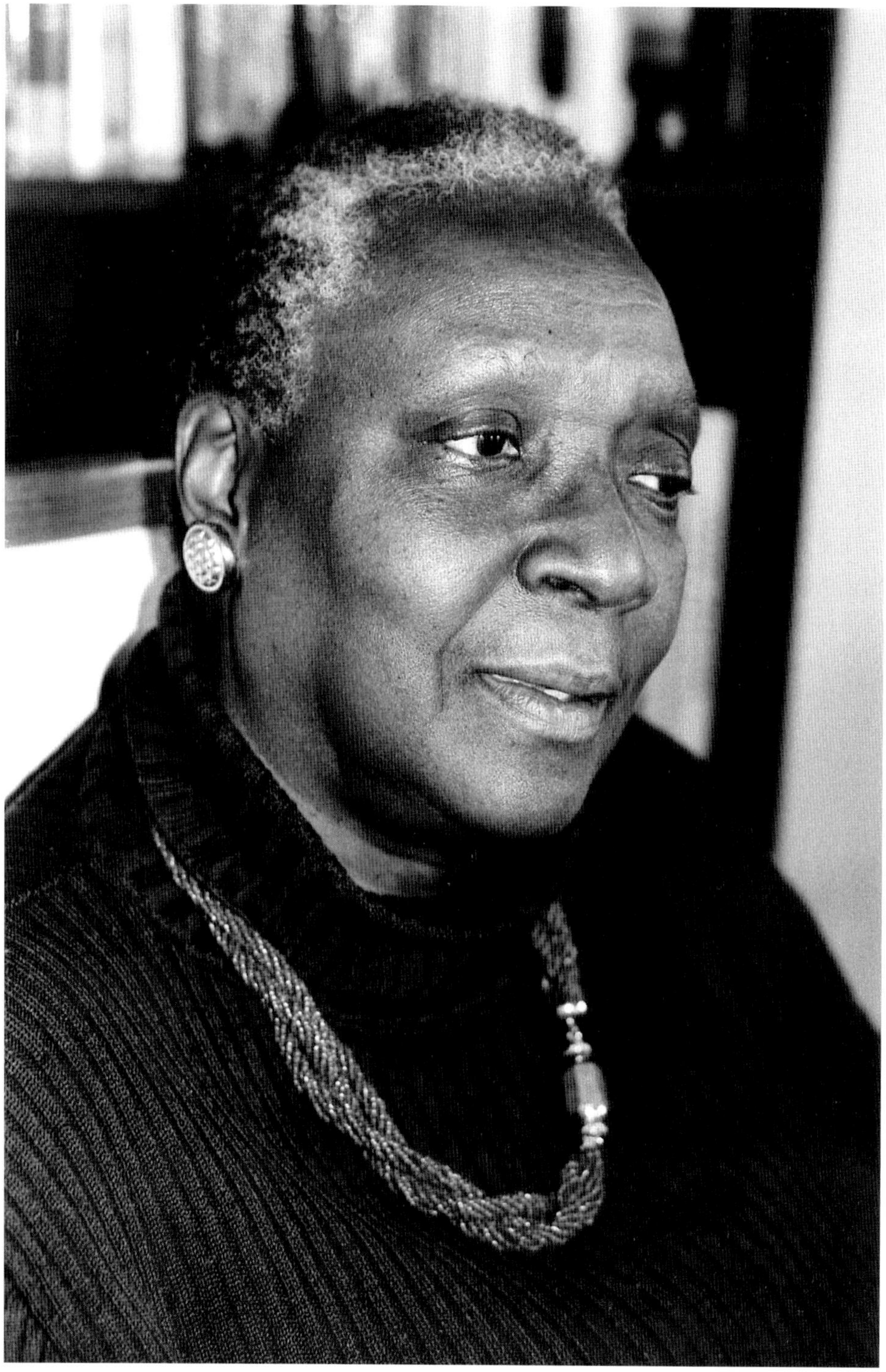

THE PHOTOGRAPH

While in Paris I endeavored to study for a B.A. in classics, to keep my father happy. My classes bored me. French seemed to me as dead a language as Latin or Greek. Literature conjured up merely ghosts from a dusty, alien past. So I skipped classes. I hung about the cafes. I walked down to the banks of the Seine and gazed at the flow of gloomy water. I had made friends with a bouquiniste who specialized in books from overseas, a vague term covering anything which was not French. I had already bought from him a woodcut by Andre Thevet of a "Tupinamba cannibal feast" dated 1522 as well as a first edition of Joseph Conrad's *Heart of Darkness* inscribed "with love" to a certain Daniel.

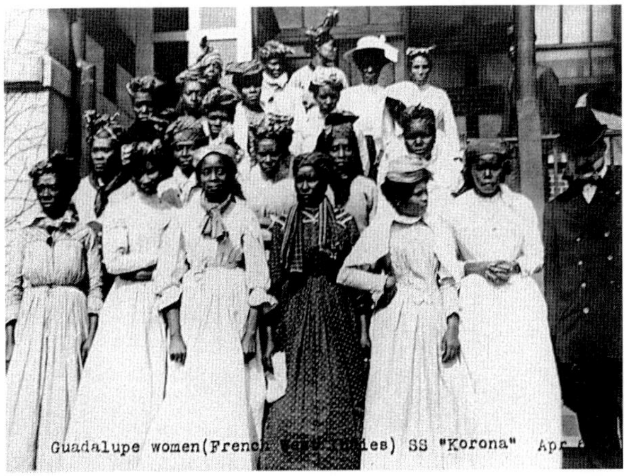

One day he showed me this photo. April 1931. A group of twenty young Guadeloupean women arriving at Ellis Island. Dressed in Creole costume. Wearing the traditional madras head ties. Smiling bravely at the camera. Not a man by their side.

What America had they come to discover? What misery, what distress carefully hidden under the frills and flounces had sent them drifting so far from their own shores?

This photo has followed me in my travels like a fetish. It has been with me in Berkeley, Charlottesville and Cambridge. And today twenty pairs of eyes still stare at me from the wall of my Manhattan apartment, revealing nothing of their mystery...

Maryse Condé
Novelist / Playwright

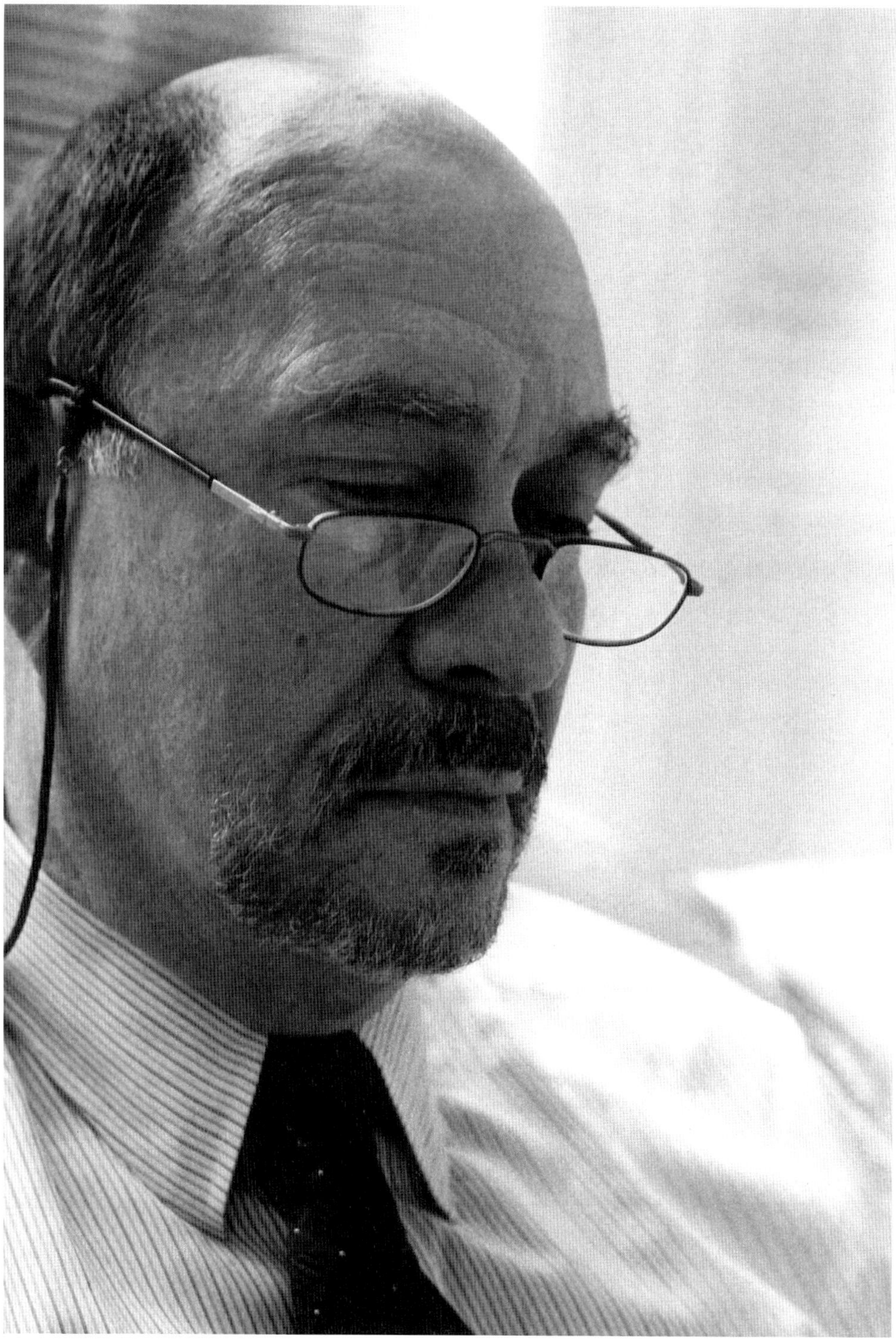

LONE COWBOY

It was at just 7 or 8 that I intuitively realized that my family was fairly nuts, and that I needed a way to survive the maelstrom at home, without losing my mind and while maintaining a reasonable front. The answer came naturally: reading and baseball. What better way to avoid the Sturm und Drang of our household? More to the point, what better way to lose myself than in the geometry and rhythm of baseball or in the perceived and felt reality of fiction.

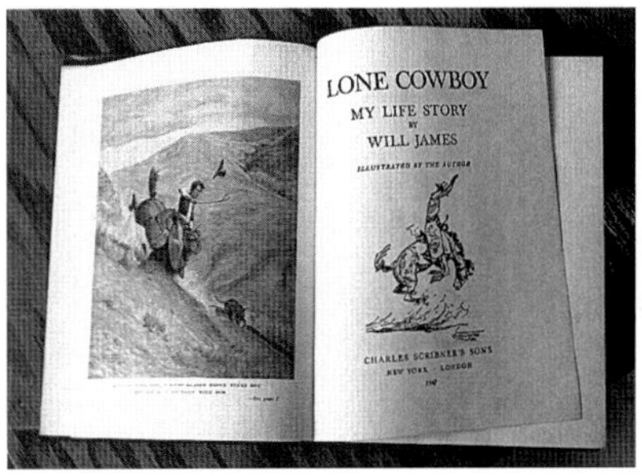

Few experiences have equaled the delicious feeling of sunlight becoming twilight becoming shadow while shagging fly balls spotted above the trees or of being immersed in the fortunes of *The Black Stallion* or Jim Hawkins (*Treasure Island*) or scrutinizing Will James' drawings in his book, *Smoky The Cowhorse.*

Winter meant time in the library after school poking around and finding new things to read. Knowing Will James, I was thrilled to discover that his book *Lone Cowboy My Life Story*, illustrated by the author, was part of a handsome (read classy) new series of illustrated hardback books published by Charles Scribner's Sons. At the time, this series of books with their striking black covers, stiff clear plastic dust jackets and tipped-in color cover illustrations were the hippest, most elegant, most extravagant things I had ever seen. I desperately wanted to own this book, all 431 pages and 42 illustrations (eight in color) with "many of the author's pen sketches of cowboy life... used as head and tail pieces throughout the book without titles".

Thirty-five-cent-a-week allowances were saved, money from odd jobs around the neighborhood was hoarded and in due course James' *Lone Cowboy My Life Story* had an honored place in my room. The book was read, re-read, and then studied; color plates were pored over and powerful, lifelong attachments were made to some of the images (many years later I discovered that these are James'paintings).

Will James was a poorly educated man, a drifter, a vagabond, a cowboy – one of the last of a dying breed. His story could not have been further from the one that was being assumed for me – and, probably, by me. But through his work, his art, I met someone who had a talent and used it, who did what he loved and who was his own man – qualities which set him apart from anyone I had ever known.

Stephen Rosenberg
Art Dealer

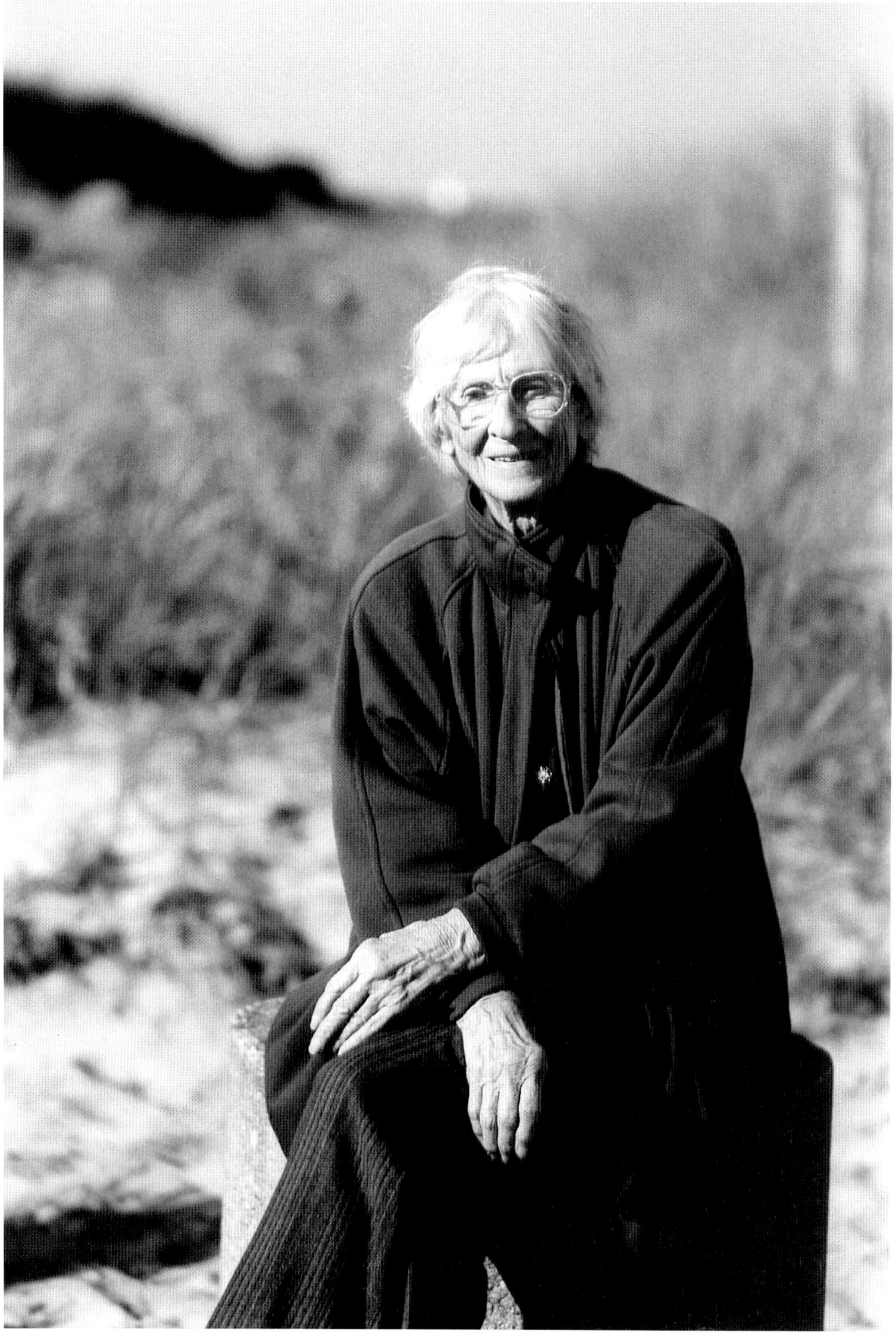

THE SEA-GULL

Regal-Sea-Gull Alert

They love to play in the sky, flying into winds that carry them up into the clouds, then down to skim the surface of the ocean.

They accompany the fishing fleet back in the late afternoon, feasting on scraps thrown from the boats and calling loudly to the fishing families to start setting the table.

When the tide is out they go clamming, flying fifty feet up to drop the clam on a rocky surface to split the shell.

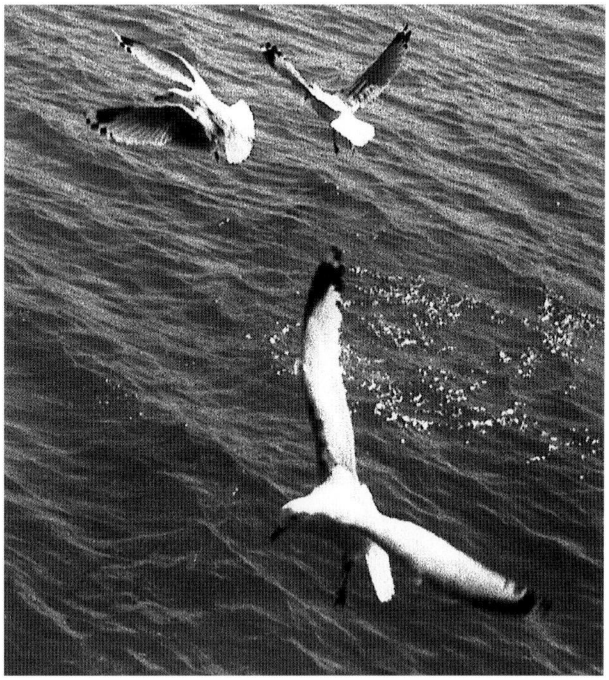

Dorothy O'Donohue
Registered Nurse

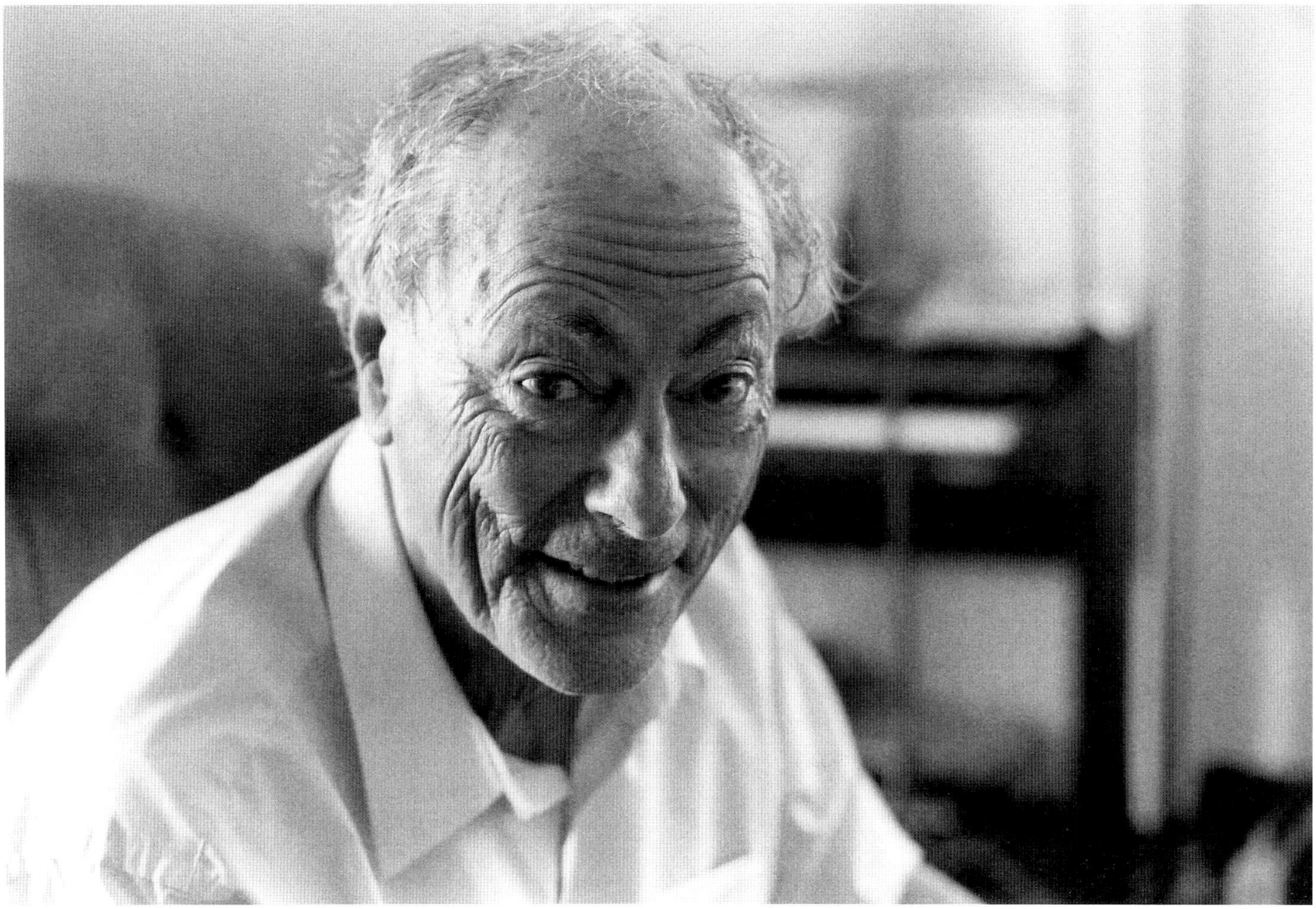

THE MUSIC SCORE

"Les bons plats se mijotent longtemps" proclaims French peasant wisdom (Good dishes must simmer a long time). How about a half century?

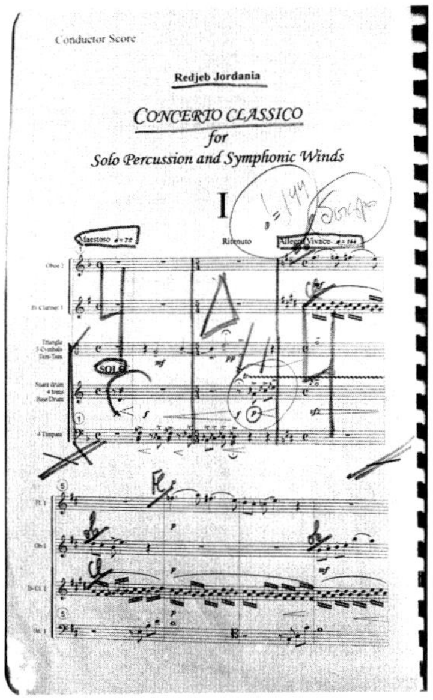

The first draft of my Concerto Classico for Solo Percussion and Symphonic Wind Instruments dates from 1951, as attested by the copyright stamp of the French royalties society SACEM.

Prokofief's Classical Symphony was the inspiration for this piece, in which I attempted to do for percussion what the Russian master did for the symphonic form. Note that this was truly an innovative work at that time, since there was then no percussion concerto in the repertory.

When I finished that first version of the concerto, however, I was not satisfied with the result, and stuck it in a drawer with intention of eventually revising it. Once in a while, perhaps once a decade, I would have a look, and think to myself: "That's not bad at all, one of these days I must finish it."

And thus, for a half century, like part of my being, the manuscript followed me everywhere I went: from Paris to Spain, from Germany to America, to Pennsylvania, Connecticut, Long Island, New York City, where, at long last, revision time finally came.

The original score had been penned by hand, each note a work of art. Fifty years later computer technology allowed me to play the parts on my digital piano and watch the score miraculously being produced by the computer printer. In this modern manner, I rewrote perhaps one quarter of part one, Allegro Vivace, and perhaps 30% of parts two and three, while part four, Allegro Molto, is 70% new.

Over the years I had heard this concerto in my head, and more recently I'd heard it played by the virtual orchestra generated by the computer. But it was not until June 2001 that I had the thrill of actually hearing my creation performed by live musicians, when my Percussion Concerto was played and recorded in Moscow by the Russian Federal Orchestra, with one of Russia's best percussionists, Alexei Amosov, as soloist and my cousin Vakhtang Jordania conducting.

It only took half a century...

Redjeb Jordania
Pianist / Music Composer

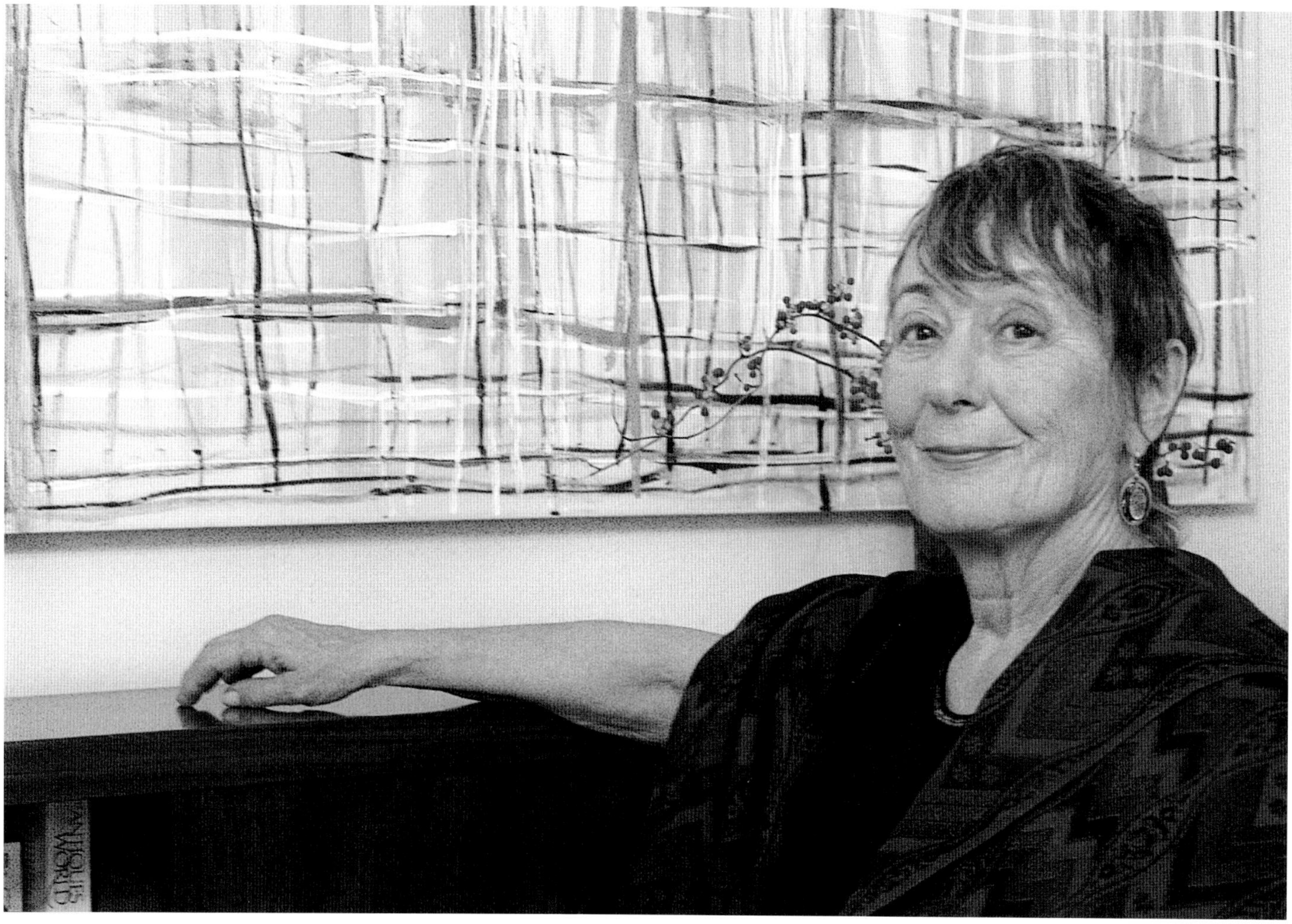

THE MUSIC FOLIOS

They stood side by side, some thirty of them, in a rosewood cabinet of the thirties – which I did not like at the time! The largest set, the "Bachs", were bound in a fine brown leather and mottled paper. Subdued and dignified. For the "Schumanns" my mother had selected greens and blues, while the "Schuberts" dark pinks matched, I thought, the melodious piano pieces. The "Chopins" were covered with tan skin and greyish-blue undulations ran across the paper like turbulent waves. I loved to sneak under the babygrand while my mother played Chopin. I would imagine her fingers running across the keyboard. The sounds swirled around me, sometimes detached one from the other, sometimes swelling like an approaching storm.

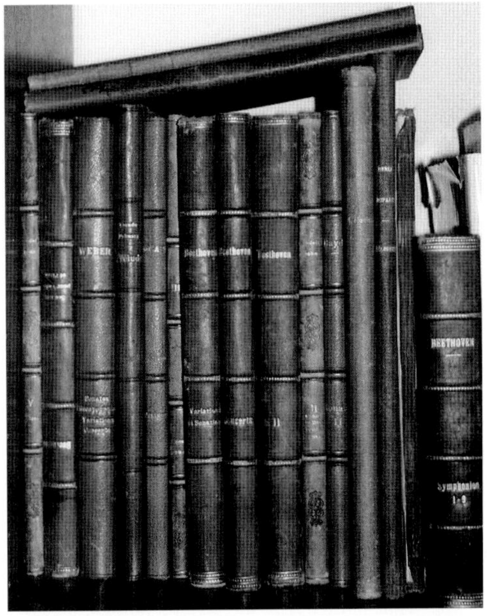

She had spent the little money she made teaching piano to have these scores bound, carefully choosing the colors and the hides. But the modern composers, those of the twentieth century, were not granted the royal mantle. They were stored in large blue cardboard files which she had labeled in her so recognizable handwriting: Ravel, Debussy, Vincy d'Indy, Milhaud, Poulenc, Albeniz, Mompou, and many more. Curiously, Satie was not among them. Had she lost her taste for the splendors of bindings or had a rather conventional marriage put an end to such "extravagant" spending?

The volumes have been scattered among her children. The pages of the C.F. Peters Leipzig edition have not yellowed much nor have the bindings suffered much from ageing. The few that are mine have followed me on the American continent. Whenever I stroke the back of one I am reminded that once there was a young free-spirited woman who had no prescience of the terrible events that was to drive our family out of Lorraine.

Madeleine Hage
University Professor

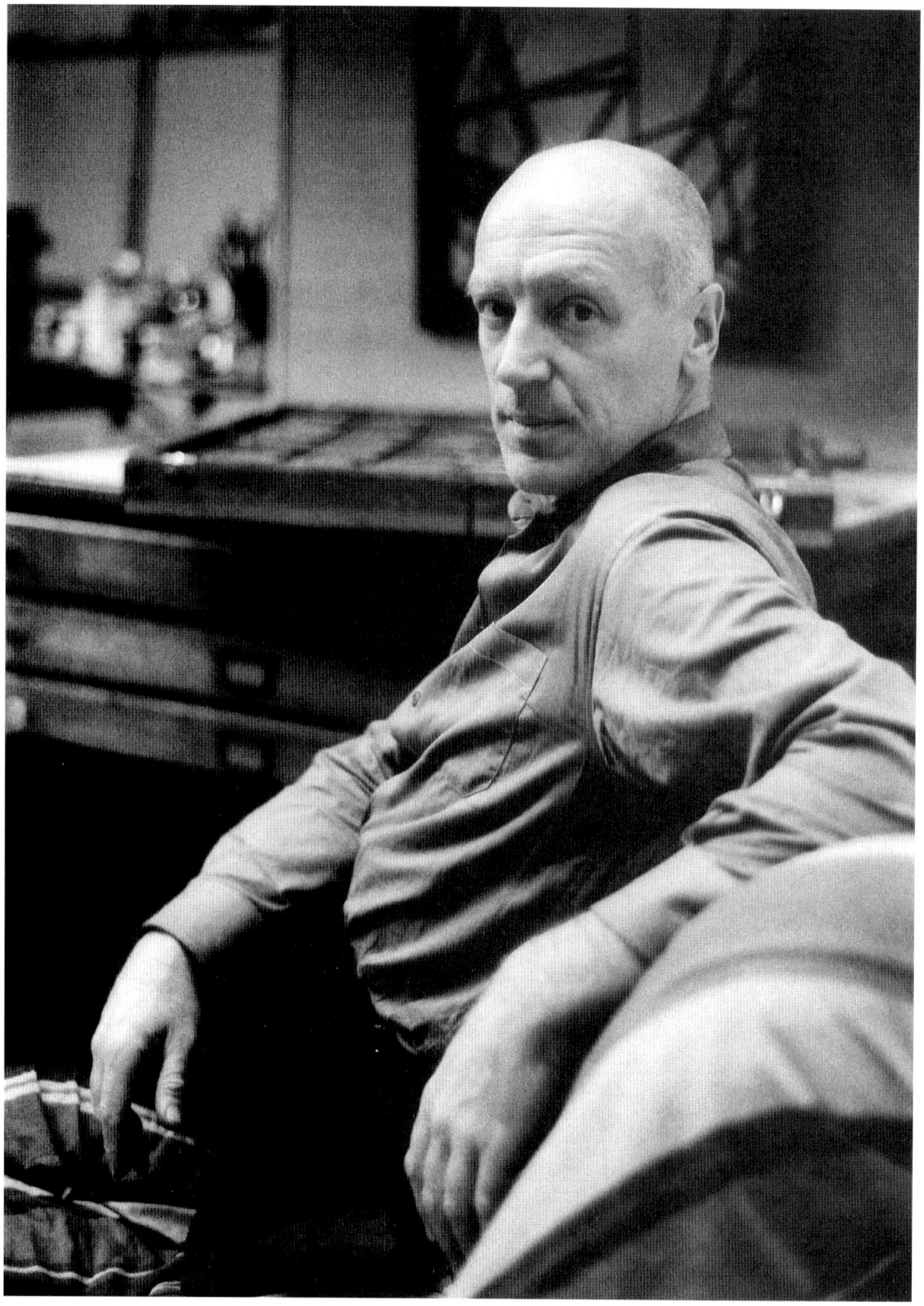

THE GOLF SOCK

JULY 17, 1934 Born Long Beach, N.Y.

JULY 18, 1934 Career choice (helped by father DENTIST) DENTIST

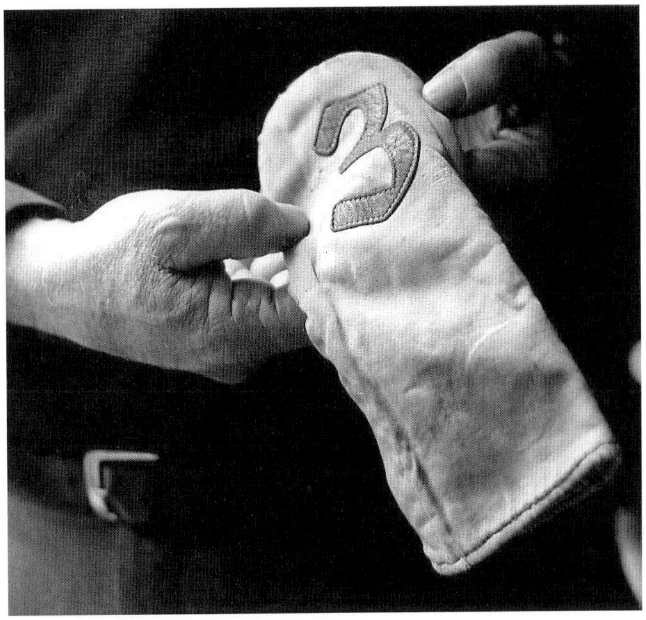

Many years of education follow: Lafayette College '56 leave '55 Hurry Hurry off to Dental School you have a job to do.

JULY 14, 1957 Chose a Bride with Father's Blessings.

JULY 1959 Chose a Dental Partner with Father's help and Blessings.

Ten years into building a successful practice, a marriage and two children, and a Father forever present, I suddenly realized I had a Mom. So little time was spent together during those many years, we hardly knew each other.

JULY 1969 I gave my Mom a Car. I was successful and I think she was thrilled both with me and the car.

AUGUST 1969 Mom is diagnosed with acute leukemia, where is Father now. My mother passed away Christmas Morning 1969. The car is returned to me to get rid of and it contains nothing but the golf sock you now see. I wish I could have had more of Her, but you see I had to Hurry On with the things that had to be gotten.

My Loss.

Don Thaler
Dentist / Emergency Medical Technician

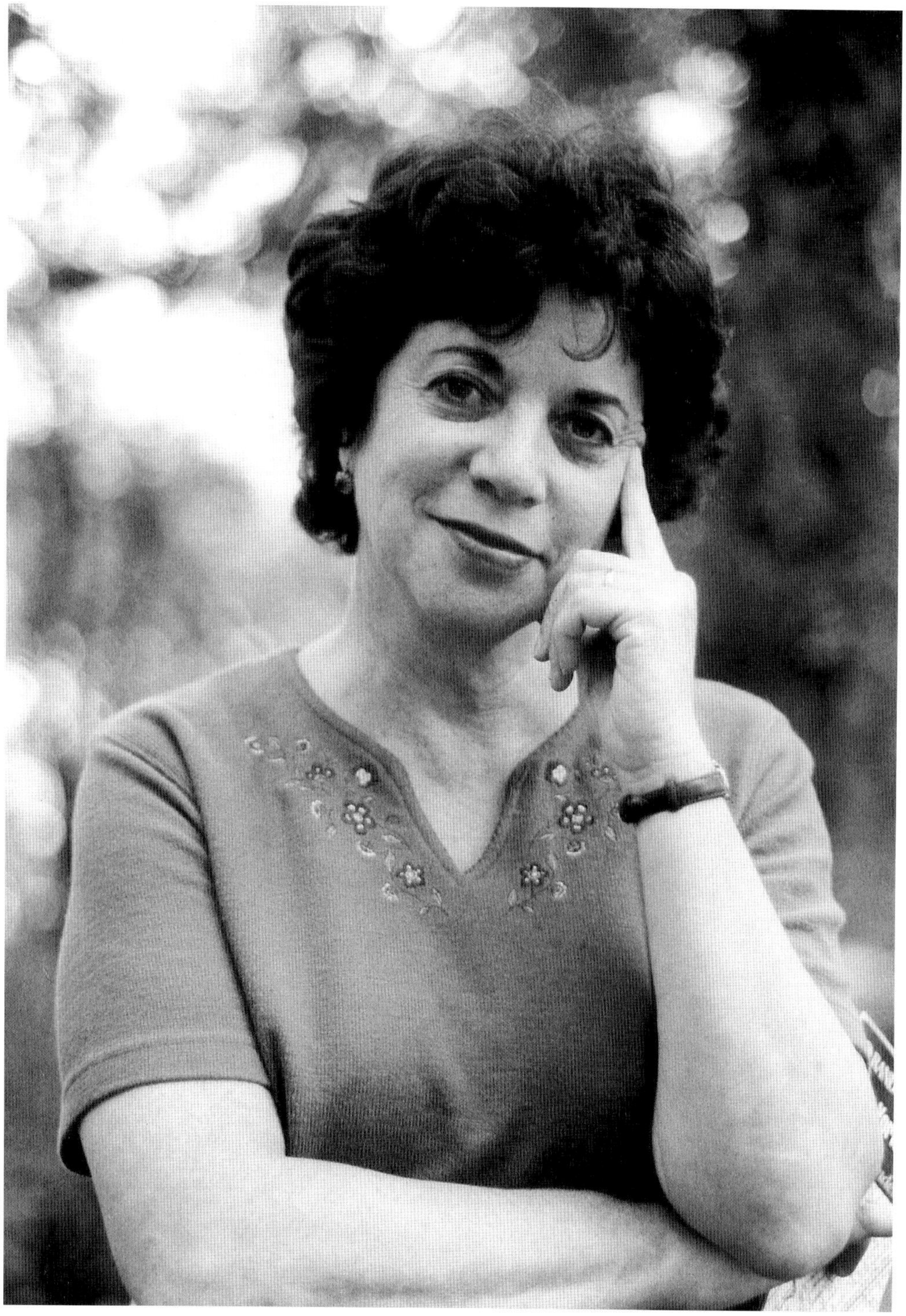

IN MEMORY OF: ALBERT CASSELL (1914 – 2000)

From: Albee 1914 To: Maxime@ aol.com
Date: March 11, 1998

Dear Maxime,
Humphrey has been sick again. That is why I haven't been able to write to you sooner. By the way, did you know that your mother gave you a boy's name? She got confused as usual. Maxime Weygand (a man), was the name of a famous French general in WWI. So, if you have identity problems, you know whom to blame. You have to excuse her. You are indeed a French cat but you are not a Maxime, rather a Maxine!!
Love, Grandpa Daddy

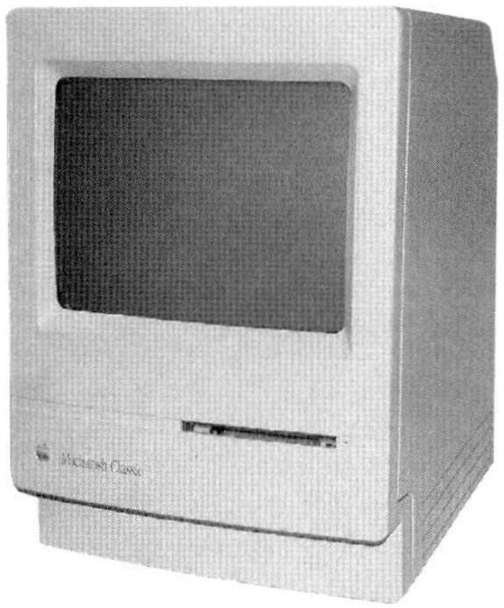

Maxime was our cat, our female cat, our long lost Delphine's sister. Humphrey was my father's Mac Classic, my daughter Madie's computer at Columbia until she graduated and gave it to her Grandpa..

Humphrey changed my father's life. At 80, he, who had never learned to type and had been "technologically challenged", in a big way, his entire life, conquered Humphrey. And with Humphrey, he tried for the first time in his life to really express himself in writing. He emailed Maxime in France. And Maxime emailed back.

We, in the immediate family, all knew about his intelligence, his scrupulous honesty and attention to fact, his incredible passion for American history and baseball (especially Brooklyn Dodger memorabilia), but his whimsical side took us all by surprise and especially Maxime.

He must have realized that Maxime would not put up with what were regarded in the family as tyrannical religious demands and required consistent good humor. He was consistently tolerant and good humored.

He must have realized that Maxime needed to be amused, not harangued. He amused her greatly with observations both philosophical and acutely ironical. He must have realized that Maxime needed some sort of show of affection from her Grand Pa Daddy. He was affectionate and considerate towards her – traits with which he was not generally identified.

He must have realized that Maxime thrilled to his subtle and perceptive commentaries on her many weaknesses. He was very, very subtle (again not his best known trait) and playfully critical on all the old subjects of contention.

Humphrey, that charming and discrete machine (Apple at its most adorable) took on a life of its own giving my father, a new voice at the end of his life, that of "Albee1914". It helped him to express things he never was able to express before, in a few inspired words of reconciliation and gave him a bit of fun in that last period when fun was so hard to come by.

Joan Cassell Dassule
Art History Professor

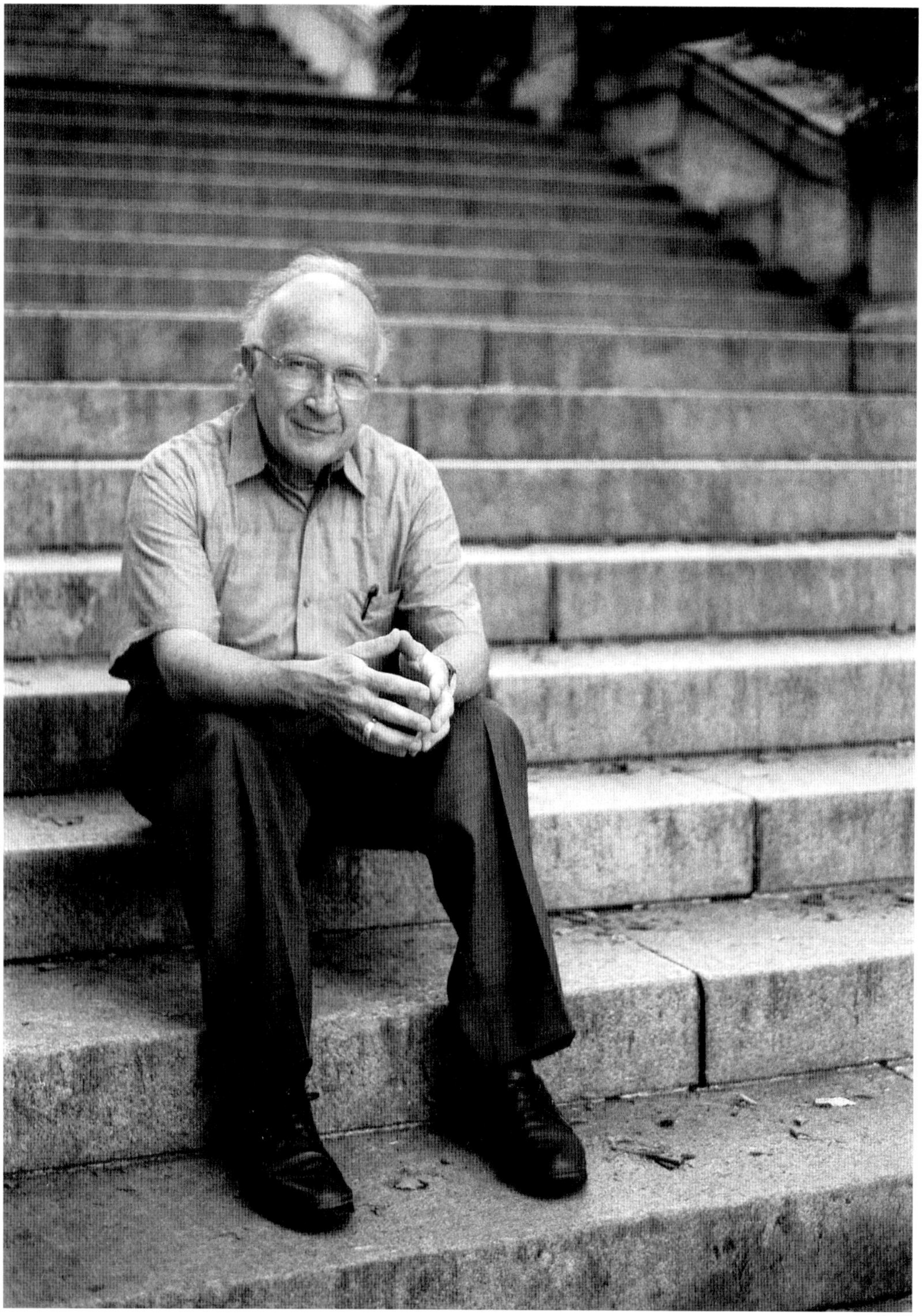

MME LAVOISIER'S NÉCESSAIRE

About twenty years ago David Corson was showing to me Cornell's fantastic Lavoisier collection. Finally, he put before me a book-like object, its title "*Histoire des Theatre.*" David said, "It's not a book."

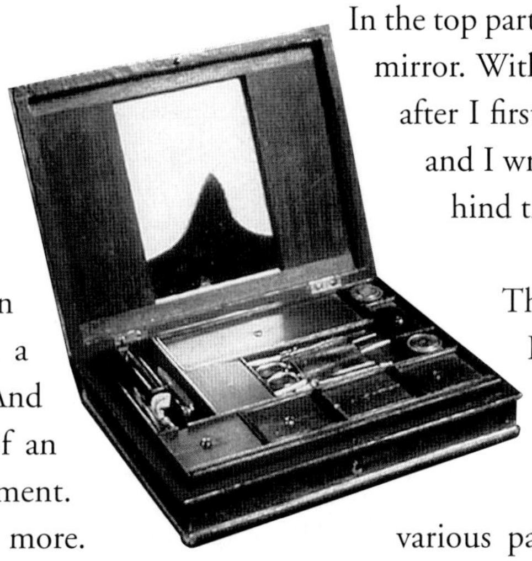

It wasn't. It was a cleverly designed *nécessaire*, Marie Anne Pierrette Paulze Lavoisier's travel kit. Opened, you see many intricately covered compartments. In them are sewing things – thread, a thimble, a darning egg, needles. And all the cosmetic accoutrements of an eighteenth century lady of refinement. Which Mme. Lavoisier was, and more. Underneath a tray is some stationery. The *nécessaire* is lined with marbled paper, there is an *etiquette* of the Paris shop that supplied it "*A la Bonne Feuille Anglaise*" (maybe the English provenance explains the misspelled faux-book title).

In the top part of the "book" is a jagged, broken mirror. With a space behind it. Twenty years after I first saw the *nécessaire*, Carl Djerassi and I wrote a play in which the space behind the mirror takes a star turn.

The first time I saw the *nécessaire*, I was driven to open some small vials resting in carefully crafted compartments. In them were dried traces of cosmetics, in various pastel colors. After two hundred years their fragrance was gone. But I could feel Mme. Lavoisier's hand as she reached in to them.

Roald Hoffmann
Professor of Chemistry, Nobel Laureate

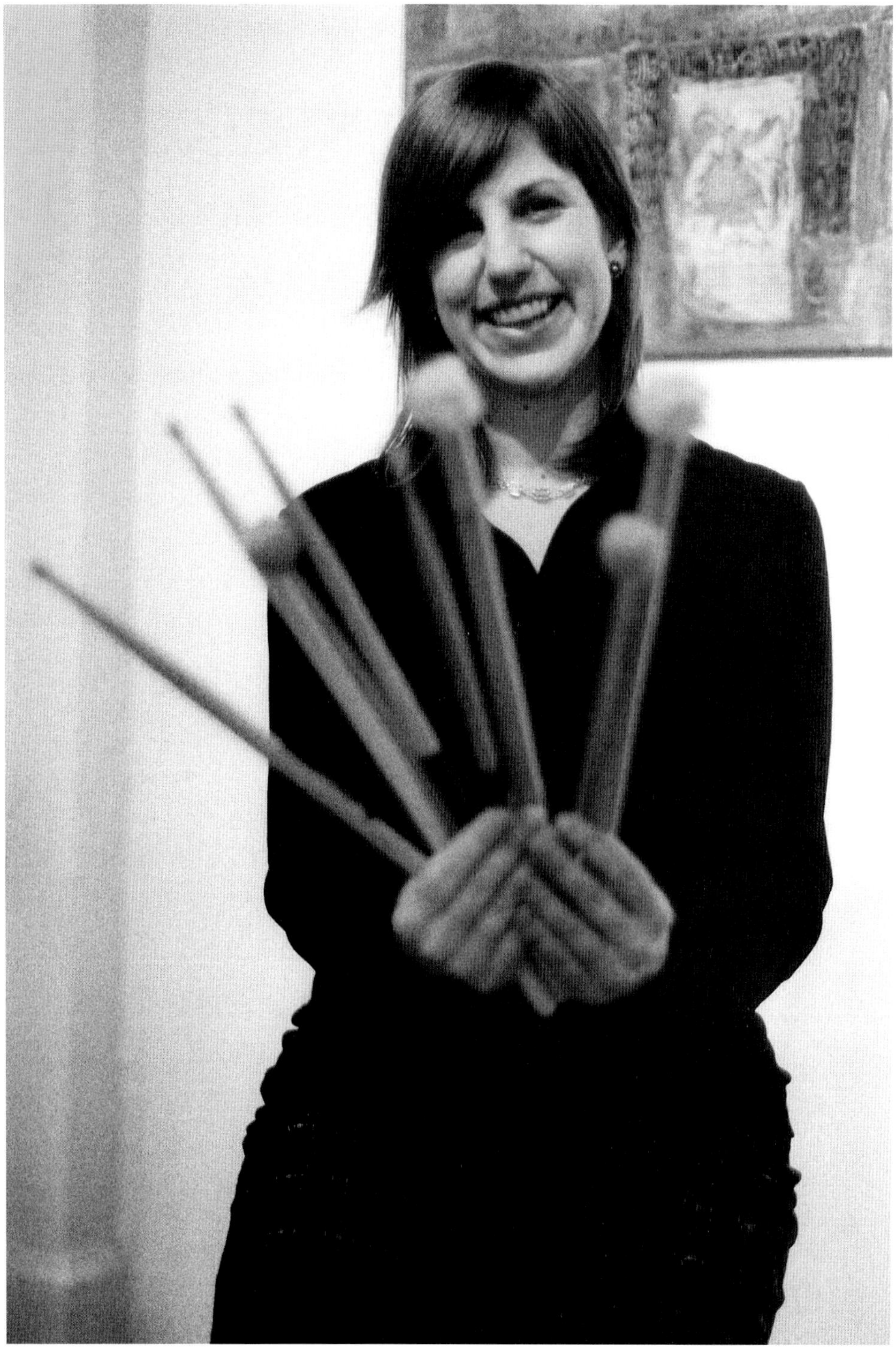

MY GRANDMOTHER'S DRUM STICKS

My grandmother's drum sticks are in a vase on my desk at work. She took drumming in College at 65, over 25 years ago. Not a common choice at retirement.

They are reminders to me to make choices on how to live.
They remind me to run full on, rather than to excuse myself from dreams and opportunity.
They remind me to live agelessly and openly without boundaries.
They remind me.

Denise Melroy
Entrepreneur

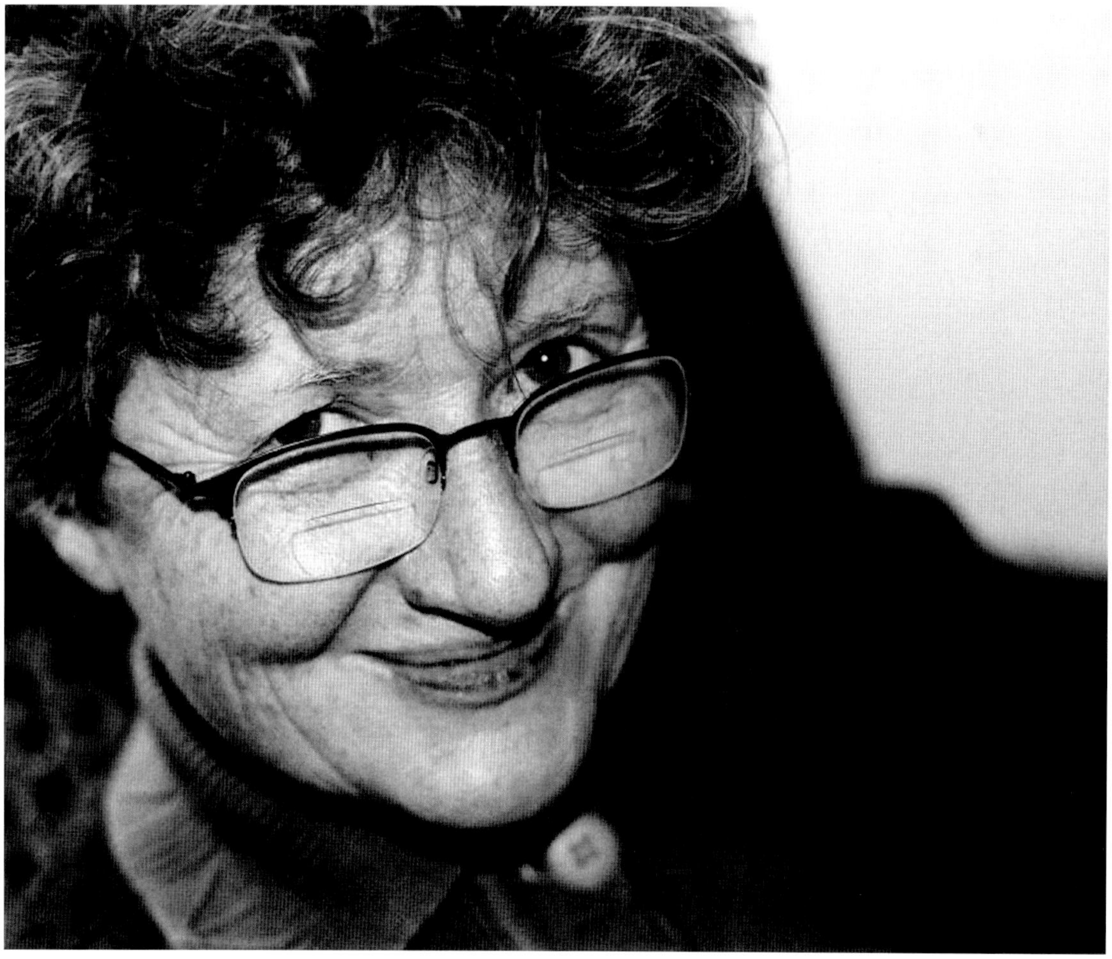

THE OLD JUG

I was born in La Puisaye, a French province where Colette, the famous writer, was born; its land of clay which has a raw and humid smell, gives shape to all kinds of pottery, humble and useful objects meant to contain water, wine or food.

My grandfather and my father collected such potteries, labeled today as "Folk Art".

Prime art alone has always attracted me. I am in tune with it, like a soul to another soul. I should say that it is like with animals, I feel an unspoken and visceral connection.

One day, years ago, I found a jug in the shape of an animal at a second-hand dealer. Its asymmetrical, open and totally innocent look caught my attention! Two tiny raised ears "dog/cat" let me imagine a close presence.

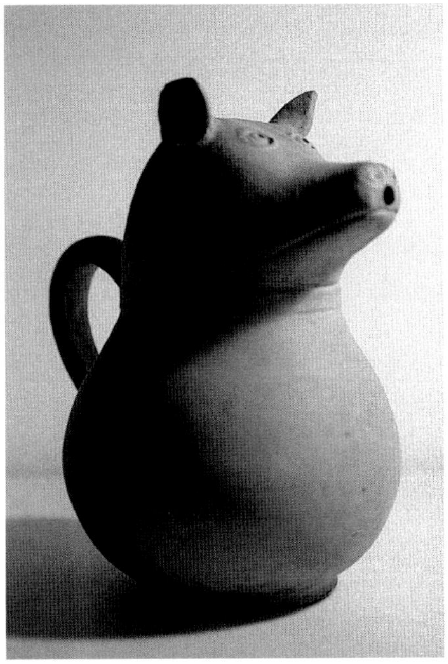

With minimal indication in the red, mat, soft and unglazed earth, its muzzle "dog/pig" pointing towards me, its tenderness spoke to me right away. Only afterwards did I notice the round part of the jug, which must have contained water.

This object is of invaluable presence, from which my sensitive and poetic work emerges. It is my hidden treasure, almost nothing, but immense in my heart.

Looking at a stone, a tree, a leaf, leads me towards a dialog on existence, and when I paint, I let appear from my unconscious, these animal and human forms, looking interrogative and generous towards our destiny.

The importance of this water jug is simply unique because undescribable.

Elisabeth Chabin
Painter

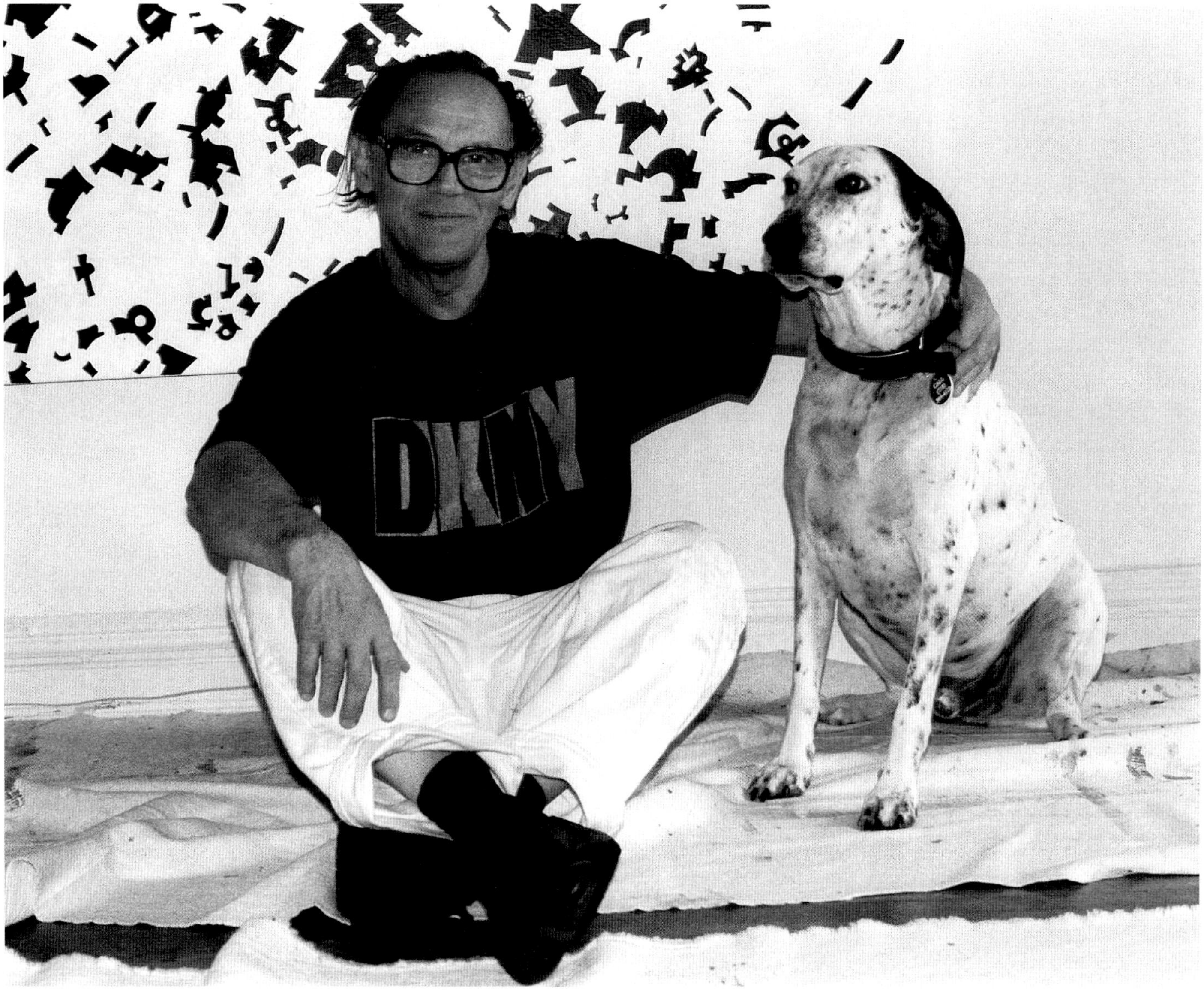
DKNY

LES BEAUX FRUITS DE FRANCE

Les beaux fruits de France belonged to my father. It encapsulates some of his life story, his passions, even some of his prejudices.

My father did not pursue the profession of his dreams. As a boy he wanted to be an aeronautical engineer, but at the age of twelve he went to work for his parents in their fields – child labor was cheap and vital for arboriculturists in those days. He set aside his disappointment and put his heart into his profession; the fruits he labored over would come to win him over as well. I remember the evenings when he pored over this book, commenting for us on the perfection of the fruits within, and on their colors and distinct flavors. He worried about American imports – our apples were certainly superior to the Golden Delicious, which would surely ruin everybody's taste! Maybe he was right. Does anyone ever see a Beurre Hardi, a Conference, a Comice, or Grand Alexandre on any market stall these days?

When I peruse the pages of this book, they evoke memories of our orchard, barn, and house: the brick wall covered by espalier pear trees; the corner reserved for gooseberry, white and red currant-bushes; and behind the water tank, a quince-tree nestled among peach-trees. The seasons rush forth, each with its own rituals: a sudden symphony of white and pink in the spring; the painstaking pruning and the delicate grafting carefully monitored by my father every fall; the bagging of infant fruits and their grotesque look, each miniature pear and apple wrapped to resist the chill of a late winter. The Frost, that dreaded threat, could ruin a crop, spoil a year of work and jeopardize the family finances, in those years, I remember my father's face drained, discouraged, and bitter.

My mother supervised our school work, but my father taught us how to cover our schoolbooks. None of us could come up to his standards. The brown kraft paper that covers my copy of *Les beaux fruits*, even after so many years, illustrates his instructions: a perfect angle, wide folds, room for opening, a notch for the spine.

There is some irony in my having chosen a book to speak of my father. He rarely spent time with us. One day, on the occasion of my fifth birthday, he gave me a chance to share the reading of a new book with him but I refused to let him – his shocked and disappointed expression is buried in my memory, mixed with guilt.

Memories and years go by. Today, I read this book with some nostalgia and regret for a bygone world and missed opportunities.

Françoise Connors
Cultural Coordinator

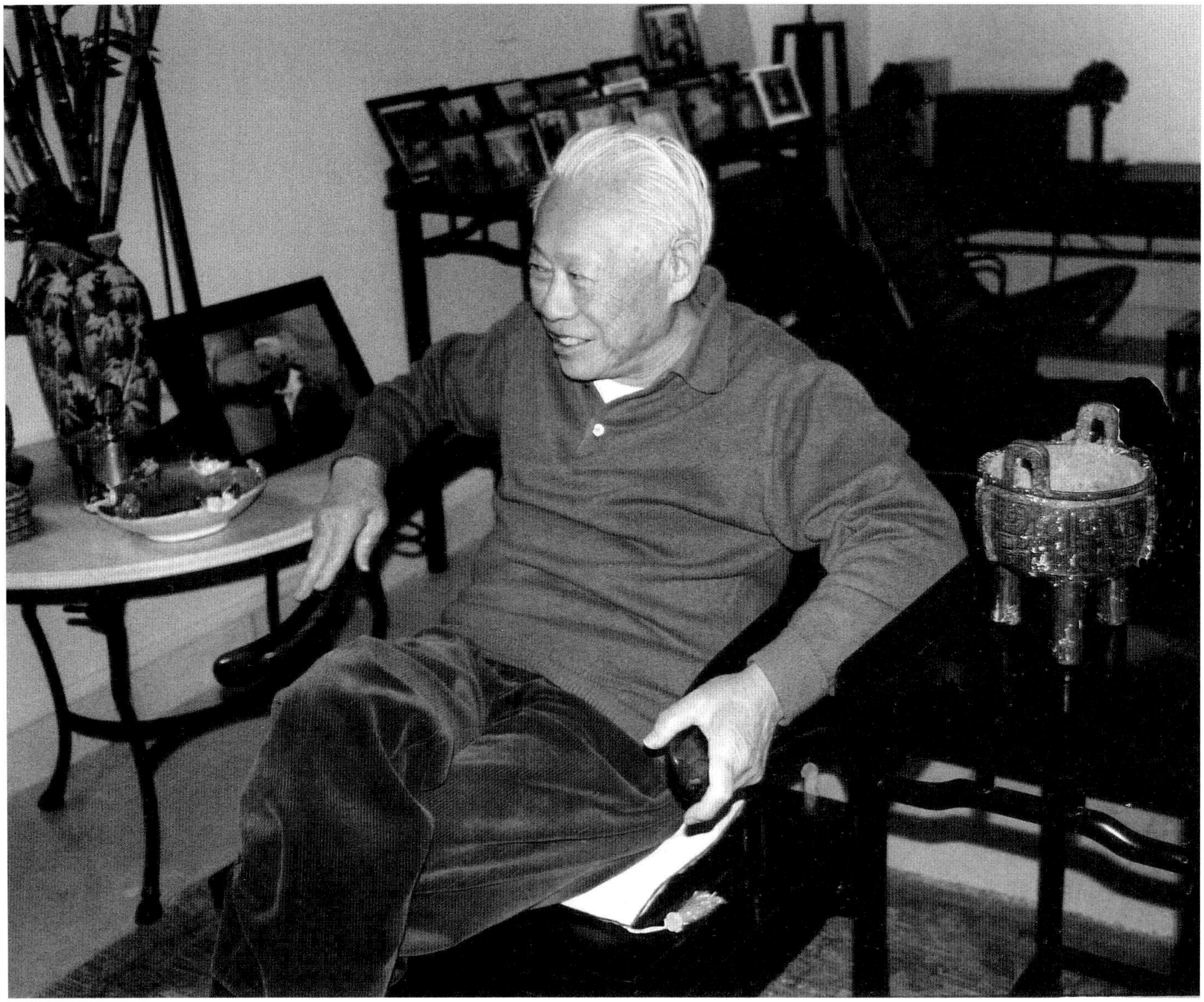

THE ANCIENT CHINESE BRONZE VASE

I cherish several Chinese bronze vases which each have their own story, but I am mostly attached to this ancient tripod bronze vase. When I was 28 years old it traveled with me from China to Paris. Prior to that time it belonged to my father who was a banker and thanks to whom I was able to follow my artistic studies.

The 11 3/4 inches high vase rests on its perfectly stable three legs; its round body has two ears and it gives a feeling of equilibrium. Originally it must have been used as a wine or food vessel. As was the custom during the Sung Dynasty, it was probably originally in a tomb with other utilitarian objects. Its green color is like that of most ancient bronze vases and its body is decorated with signs. They must be descriptive and I wish I could read into them but they keep their mystery.

This bronze vase is a presence alongside my days as a painter. It is like an old friend from my country of origin and is a reminder of the ancient Chinese culture that nourished me. It lives close to me, it is part of my background and it also reminds me of my father.

Zao Wou-Ki
Painter

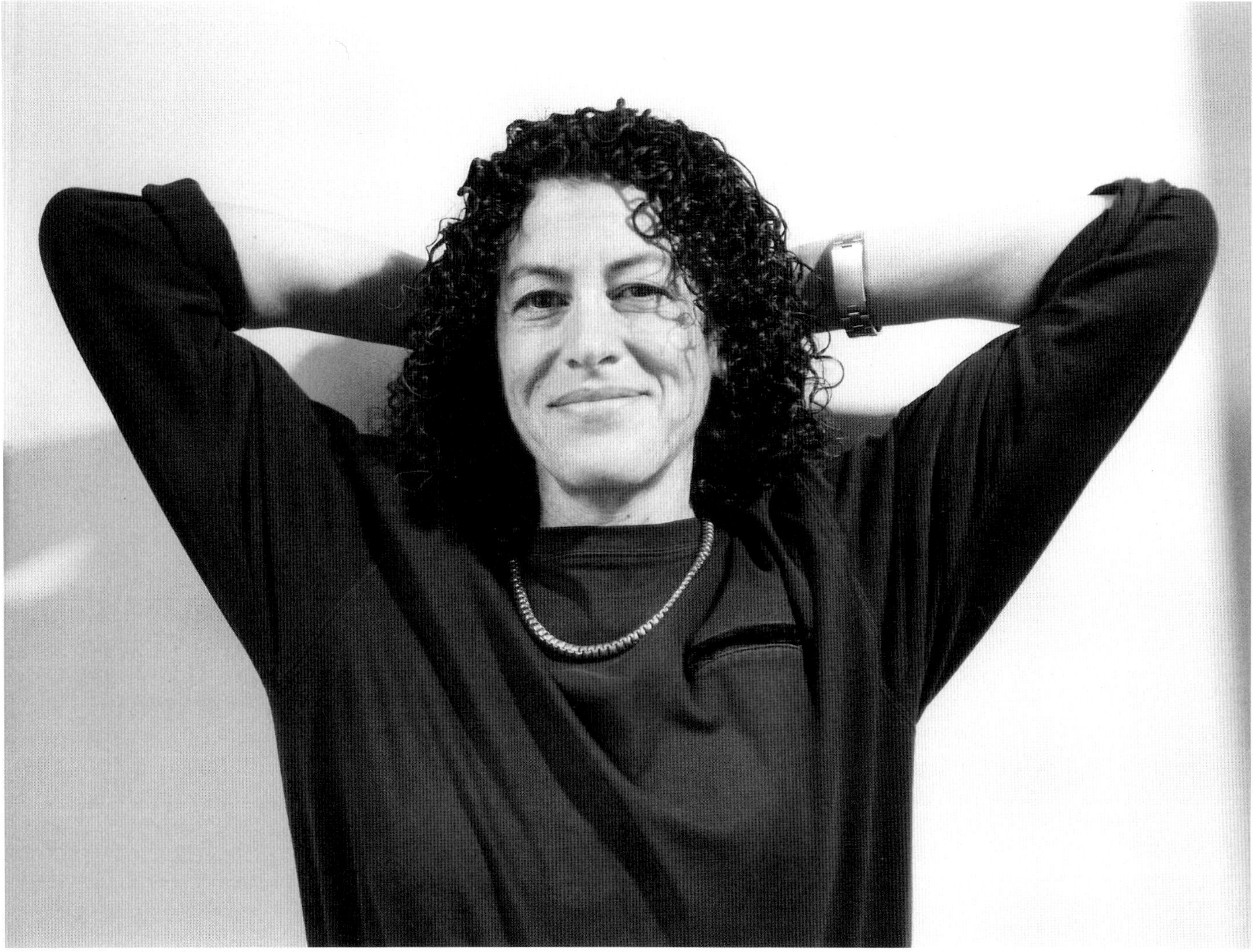

MY MOTHER'S PHOTOGRAPH

To my mother...

On December 12, 1974 my mother died of a terrible car accident in Belgium, twenty minutes outside of Brussels, heading home after work...she was fifty years old. My mother was a brave, passionate and generous woman... ahead of her time, a role model for us who were left behind.

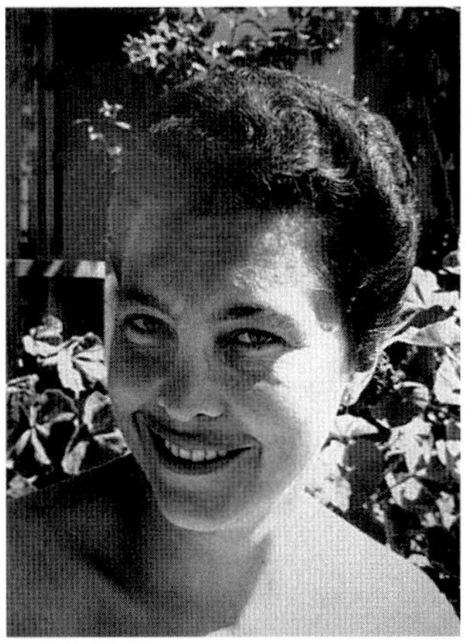

This picture of her was taken in 1960 in Mallorca, Camp de Mar, Spain, by a friend of our family while we were vacationing at my grandparents' house. This friend, too, lost his life in a car crash a few years later.

At a very young age, living in France, my mother had joined the French Resistance during World War II. Right after the war, she joined the Haganah, and left for British-occupied Palestine, as an underground nurse, helping refugees and survivors of the camps.

In 1956, alone with two young children, she decided to leave the United States, crossed the Atlantic on "L'Ile de France", and went to medical school in Brussels, Belgium. She had always wanted to be a doctor.

Unfortunately, life forced her to abandon her medical studies. Instead, she took a year of tropical nursing and was offered a job in the Belgium Congo in a territory called Gemena, in the Ubangui region. In 1958 we left Antwerp for Matadi on the "Jadotville". There, shortly after arrival, my mother learned to drive, bought a second hand car, and we left Coquihatville, driving on dirt and mud roads night and day through villages and the jungle to reach Gemena.

This photograph has traveled from Mallorca to Africa, from Brussels to France, and then to the United States. It represents a time of extraordinary history and events that have shaped my life.

Ilana Lobet
Framer

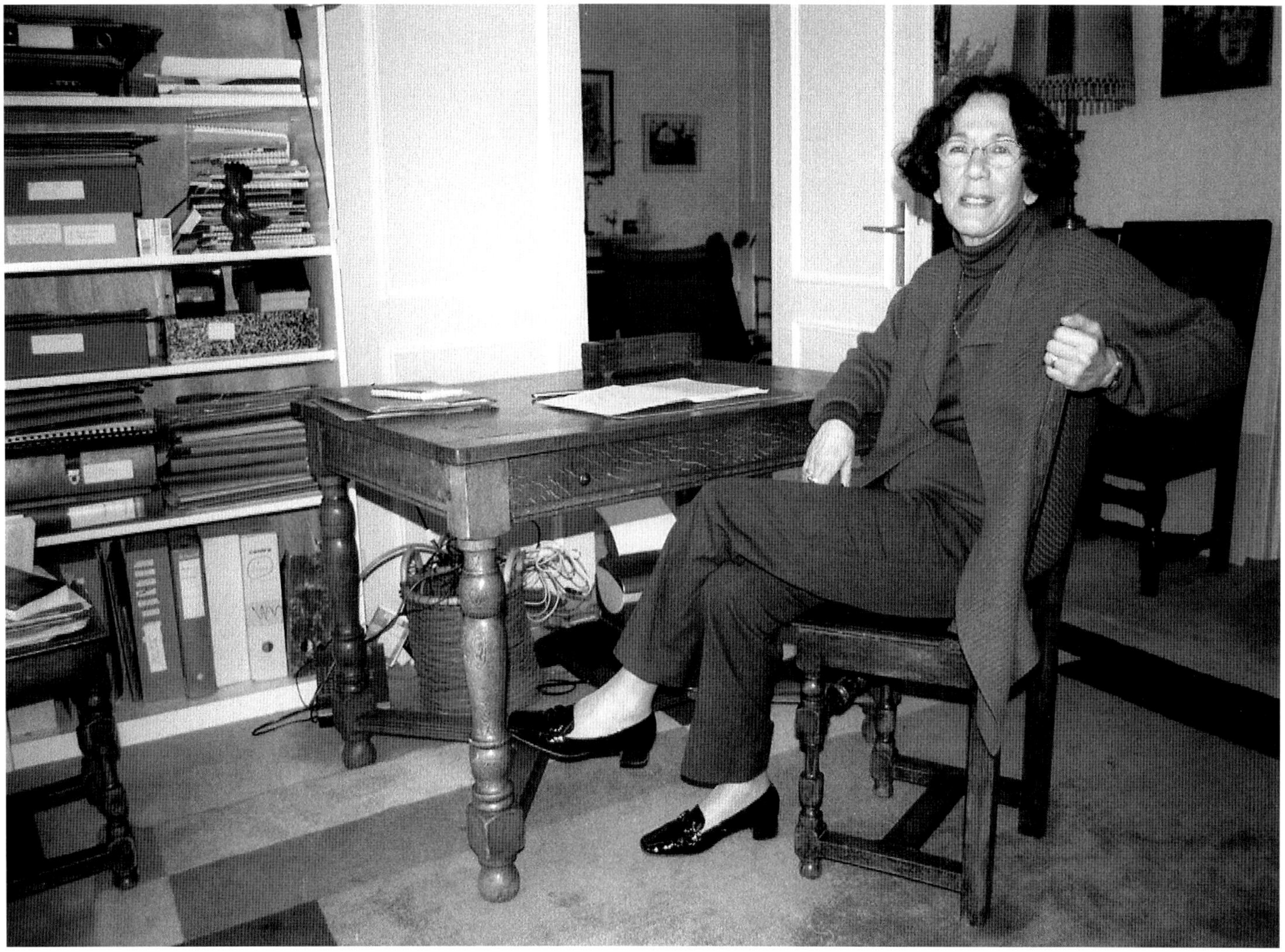

MY FATHER'S TABLE

My father sits at the table. He wears a purple cape. He had the table built specially for him. He was bored with the fake Henri II furniture of the apartment. He wanted a hard table made of old wood. On it he would be able to write comfortably.

Everyday ink poured along the oak veins. One could almost read along them the writings of my father like one can read the palm lines.

The purple cape became our dolls'clothing. Today the table has aged. How did it travel through these decades, the war, the numerous moves, and other events?

It is my turn to work on this table which speaks of yesteryears. Too bad if it vacillates on its bases. I caress it with the palm of my hand, I scrutinize its wrinkles, its injuries.

I often thought of getting rid of it. To exchange it for a more functional and modern desk. It always resists. I cannot possibly part with it.

Marie-Louise Audiberti
Writer

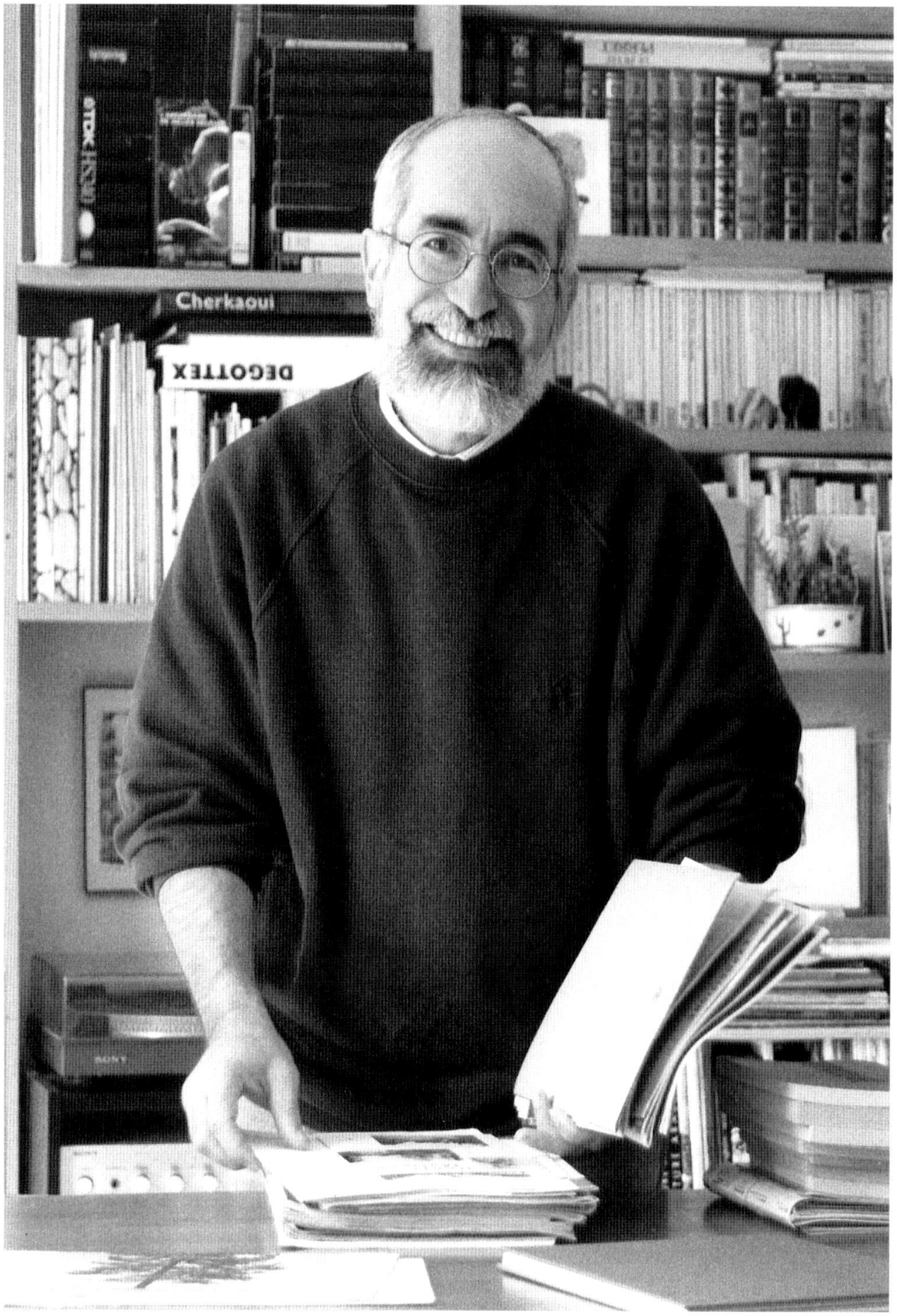
TDK
Cherkaoui
DEGOTTEX
SONY

THE HARROW

Cormeilles en Vexin, 1988. In an Antique Shop, I am struck by a splendid wooden object.

As large as a door, it is made of three thick pieces of eroded wood of similar length, but different width, slightly curved at the top, like a sled. The lower two thirds are covered with small pieces of very sharp and filed silex stones layered regularly. Because of the regularity of the layout, the object resembles a large written page. This explains why this object is so meaningful to me. Since an early age, I have been fascinated by writings. The small silex stones disposed vertically like notes on a music sheet, the ribs of the wood which have been eroded by time as well as the knars and accidents caused by intense use, make this unknown object, sitting vertically against a white wall, look like an ancient manuscript. Paradoxically, one can also look at it as a true contemporary sculpture. I already know that it is not one, though I do not yet know its history. I guess, but that is not difficult, amidst all of these old pieces of furniture and other antiquities around me, that this object must be very old, and that it was created with the utmost care.

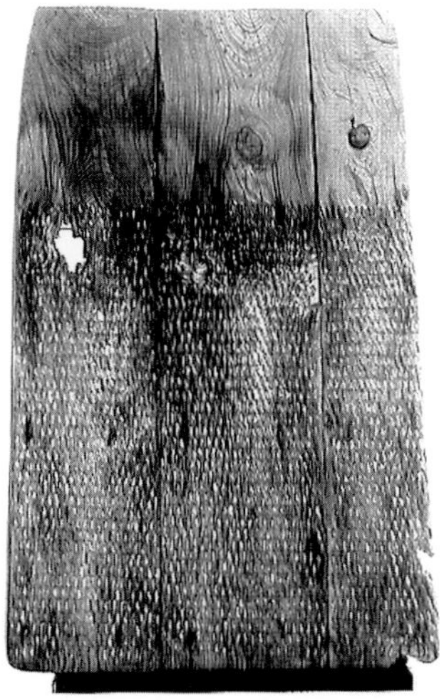

One feels that it was not only a decorative piece. No one can doubt its useful vocation; it looks like something which has been used a lot. For which noble function? In which place and when? Ageless instrument, one can feel its soul. Due to its mysterious intemporality, it speaks to me very deeply.

I get information from the dealer in antiquities, who tells me it is a farming instrument, a "tribulum", a harrow, which must have come from Spain. Indeed, it has an iron hook on the back, to allow being drawn by a yoke. The fact that it must have been dragged on ploughed land to break the clods, bury the seeds, or beat the wheat, makes it even more attractive to me and suggests almost a biblical significance. I must buy it. With the little amount of money my partner and I saved for a vacation.

This nurturing plank must have helped feed so many people!

Now that this magic sculpture sits majestically against the white wall of our living room, it continues to feed me spiritually, nurturing my work as a painter, and helping me dream.

Hamid Tibouchi
Painter

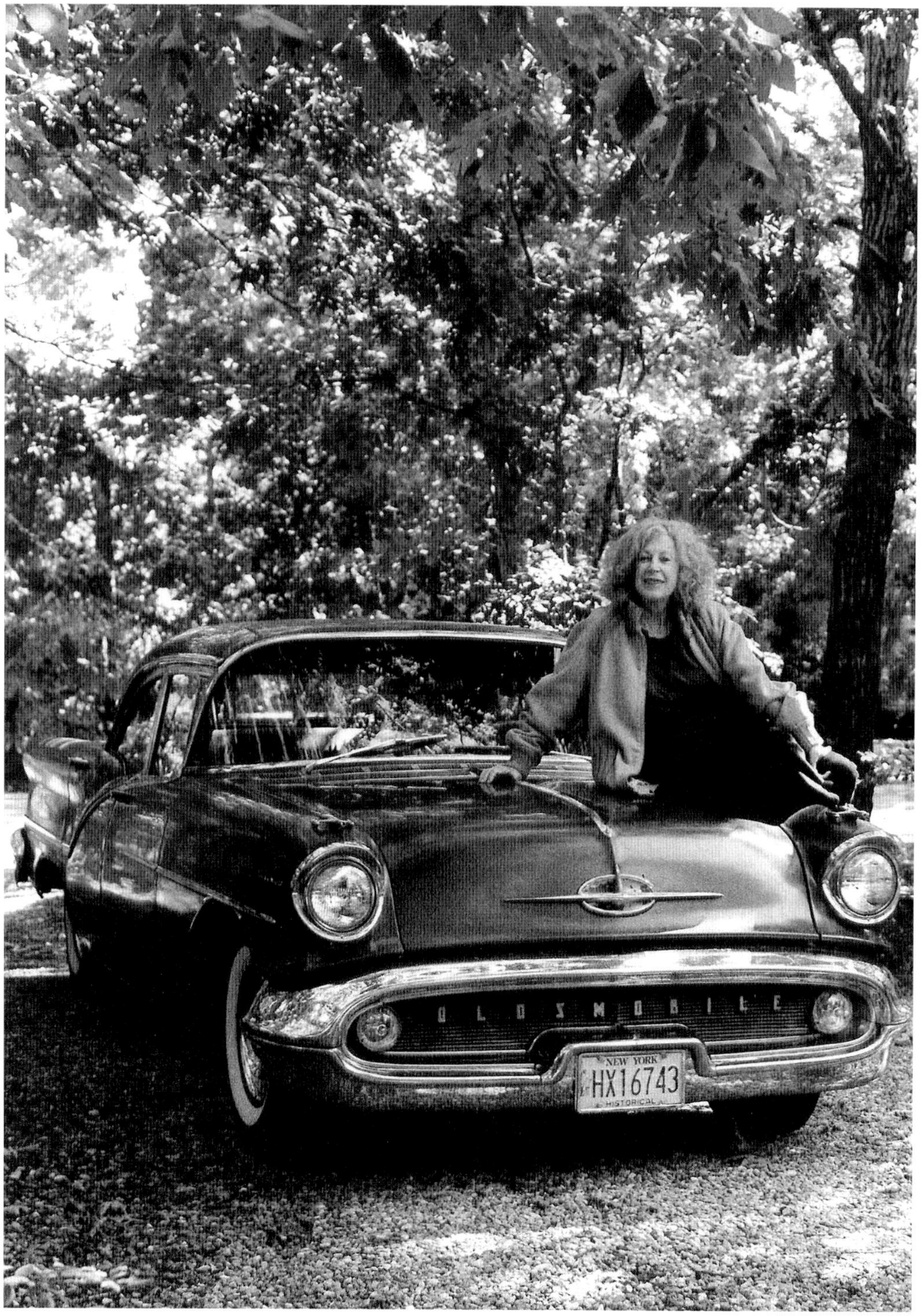
OLDSMOBILE
NEW YORK
HX16743
HISTORICAL

THE OLDS

The Olds joined our family in 1957. My father, a country doctor, had her for only a year before he died, and since my mother wasn't too keen on driving, the Olds spent most of her early years in our garage in the little Pennsylvania village of Jerome. She was our family car, a classy charcoal gray Oldsmobile '98, with lots of chrome.

Today the Olds still sports the original coat of paint – now dulled by time; and the once-shiny chrome is a bit pitted if you look closely. She is what they call a "30-yarder": that is, she looks great from 30 yards away.

I'm sure that my attachment to this car is a way of staying connected to my parents and to my hometown. The Olds gives me a sense of comfort and provides continuity in my life. And she brings me joy.

At times I think of her as an aging relative, who needs to be taken out for a drive once in a while, and who has trouble getting started if she has been sitting around too much. Nevertheless she still maintains her dignity and is able to show off her powerful motor on the road.

However, just like my mother did, I too let the Olds sit in the garage more than she should. I used to feel quite comfortable driving this car, but now at times, I am a bit intimidated. She is so huge, so enveloping. Am I shrinking? Becoming one of those little old ladies peeking over the steering wheel?

I'm not sure which of us will outlast the other. But one day, perhaps sooner that I'd like, she and I will have to part. In the meantime, it is simply fun to hear her loud powerful motor rev up, and to see people's smiles and appreciation for her beauty and for the 1950's which she represents.

Peggy Backman
Psychologist

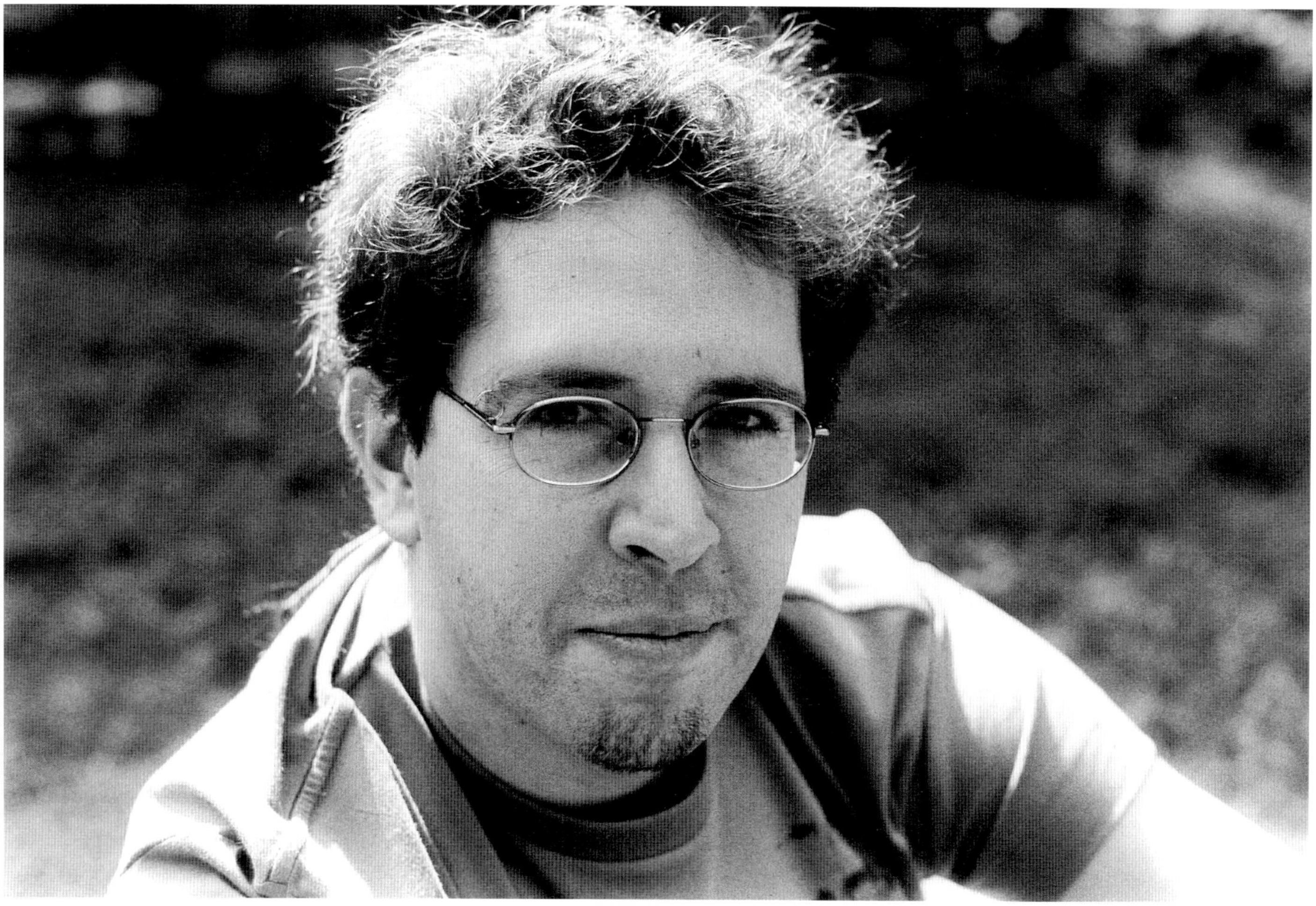

MY OLD BICYCLE

According to an old and unfounded tradition in the family, I do not have a licence to drive a car. For this reason, my means of transportation has been the bicycle since I was six years old. Until today I have had many bicycles, but I have a special love for one of them. With this bicycle, I realized my first long trip on "The Camino de Santiago". It is 780 kilometers (approximately 500 miles) long, through the north of Spain, and runs along ancient roads dating back to the Roman times. For centuries, pilgrims of the entire world have rejoiced on this magnificent road which goes through Spain, from Roncevalles (a small circus in the Navarra Pyrenees) to Santiago de Compostella, where, according to the legend, the Apostle Santiago (James) is buried.

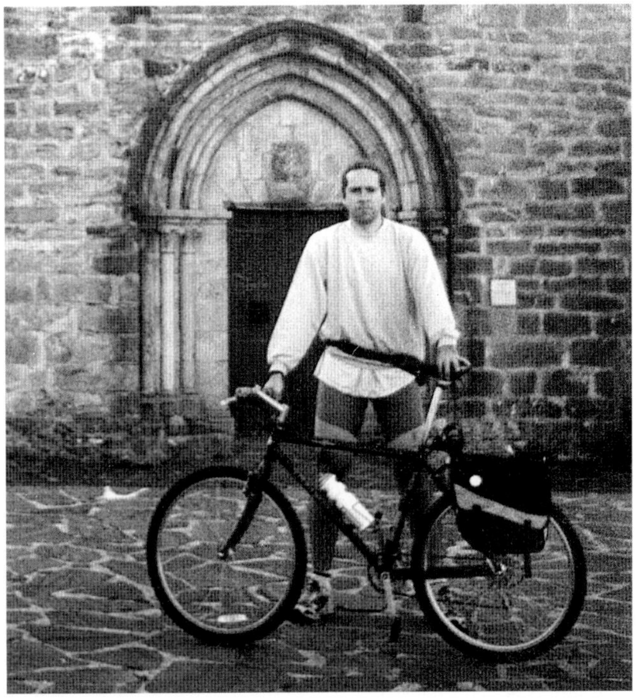

In July 2002, I started on the road with my bicycle and a friend, during nine unforgettable days through beautiful landscapes, enjoying good food, and encountering people whom I sometimes recognized, all throughout the duress of the road.

During the following months, I planned another trip, slightly longer, but, unfortunately I could not duplicate it with the same equipment: in a little more than a year, my bicycle was stolen!

Thus, my preferred object is my old bicycle (though I am satisfied with the new one), not only as a means of transportation, but as a way of evasion and liberty.

Pedro Salvador
Assistant Professor of Chemistry

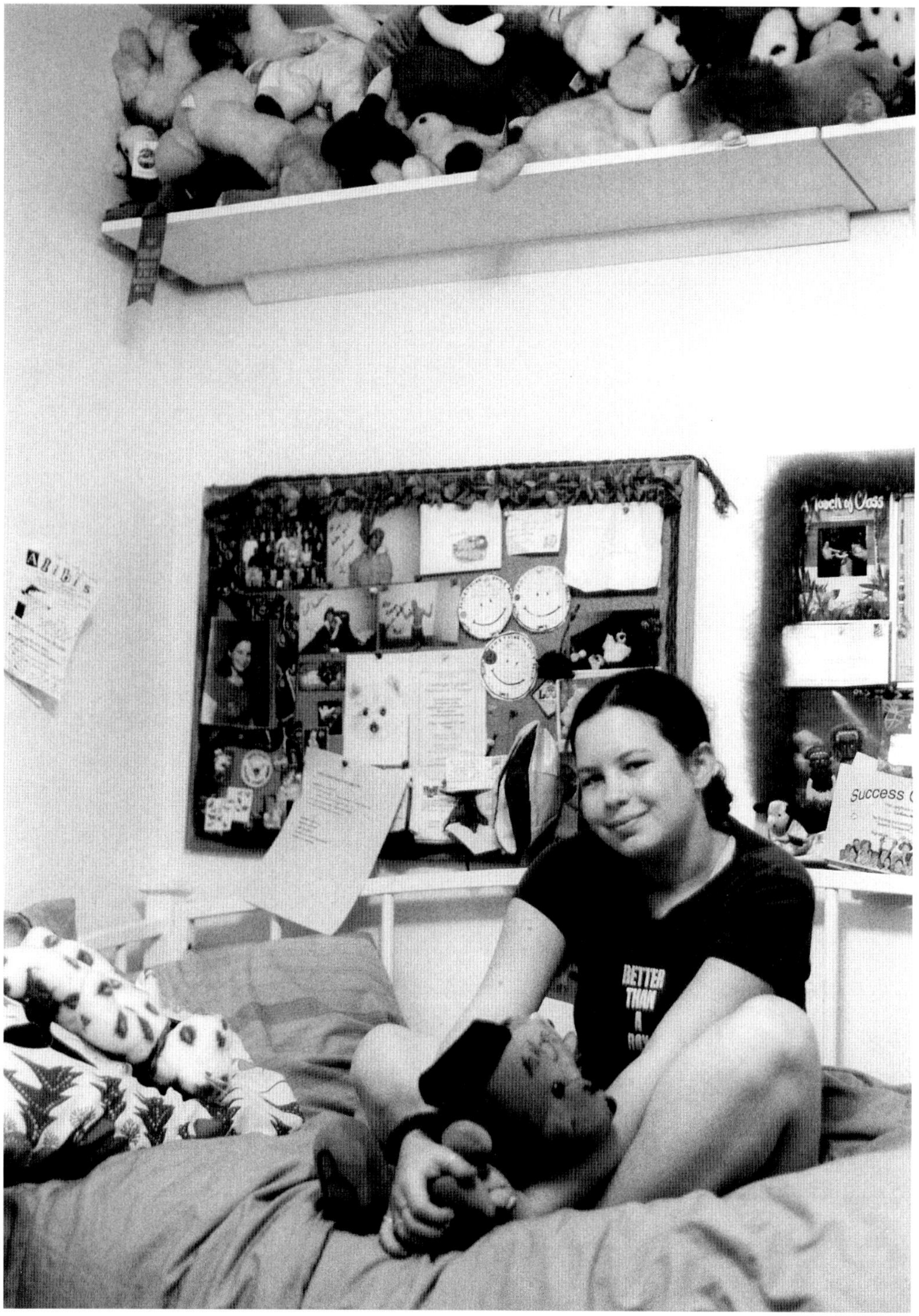
BETTER
THAN
A
Success

MY ROOM

My room is important to me because it is my own. I chose the paint color, white. I chose my bed, my table, and my stuff...

My room also has a lot of memories such as my carpet. I have owned it for my whole life. There is one spot where my friend spilled Elmers Glue when we were making hand puppets. There is also a corner that used to hold my Barbie dolls. I also have two bulletin boards that hold my memories from my first birthday to my eighth grade prom. My doors are covered with stickers, accumulated over a very long time.

Samantha Dannenberg
Highschool Student

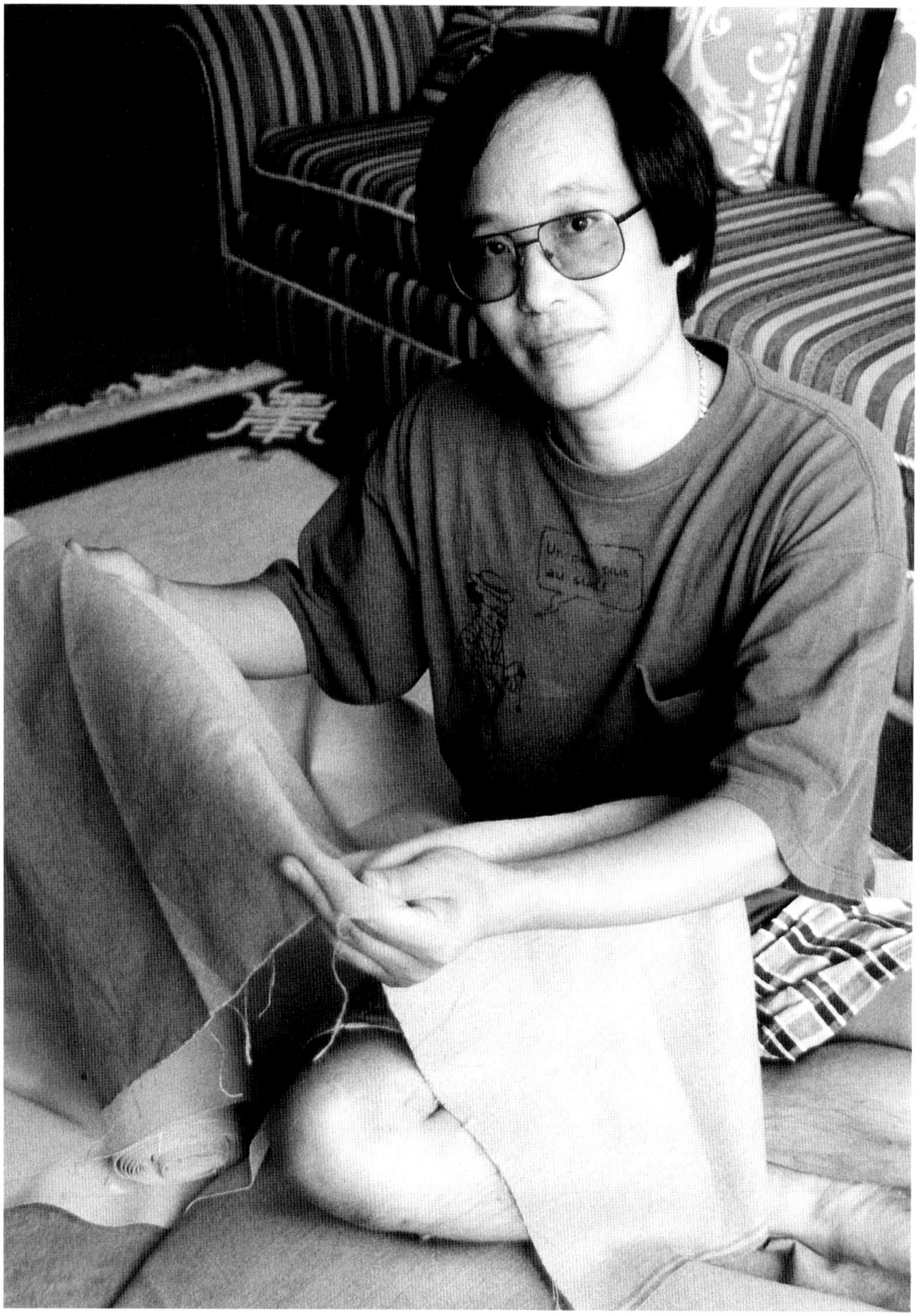

THE WHITE CANVAS

I love the rich ink falling on rice paper that absorbs it instantly. Varied and natural forms appear and I feel that I am expressing myself in total freedom. The beauty of rice paper is not merely visual, but also touches my deepest senses.

In fact, it started with the first lesson I learned from my teacher of traditional Chinese painting who used this type of ink and paper, like all Chinese painters have done for ages before him. The spontaneous enthusiasm felt by the artist when he touches the paper before starting to paint is a most familiar feeling and it remains with me to this day.

Today, the canvas plays a larger role in my work as a painter. Touching it arouses in me a desire, a need to do something with this raw material. Thanks to it, I am able to construct a painting and this frees me totally.

When I see a painting, it is the raw canvas that I admire. I see in it all the colors, the appearances, the expression of memory. It is a unique creation that is born out of this splendid raw material. It is one artist's inspiration and that inspiration comes from a raw canvas. The beauty of the completed painting transforms the raw canvas into a pure wonder.

I have loved raw canvas, as much as I have loved rice paper, ever since I first felt its beauty. When I touch it, the sensation is as fresh as ever.

Leng Hong
Painter

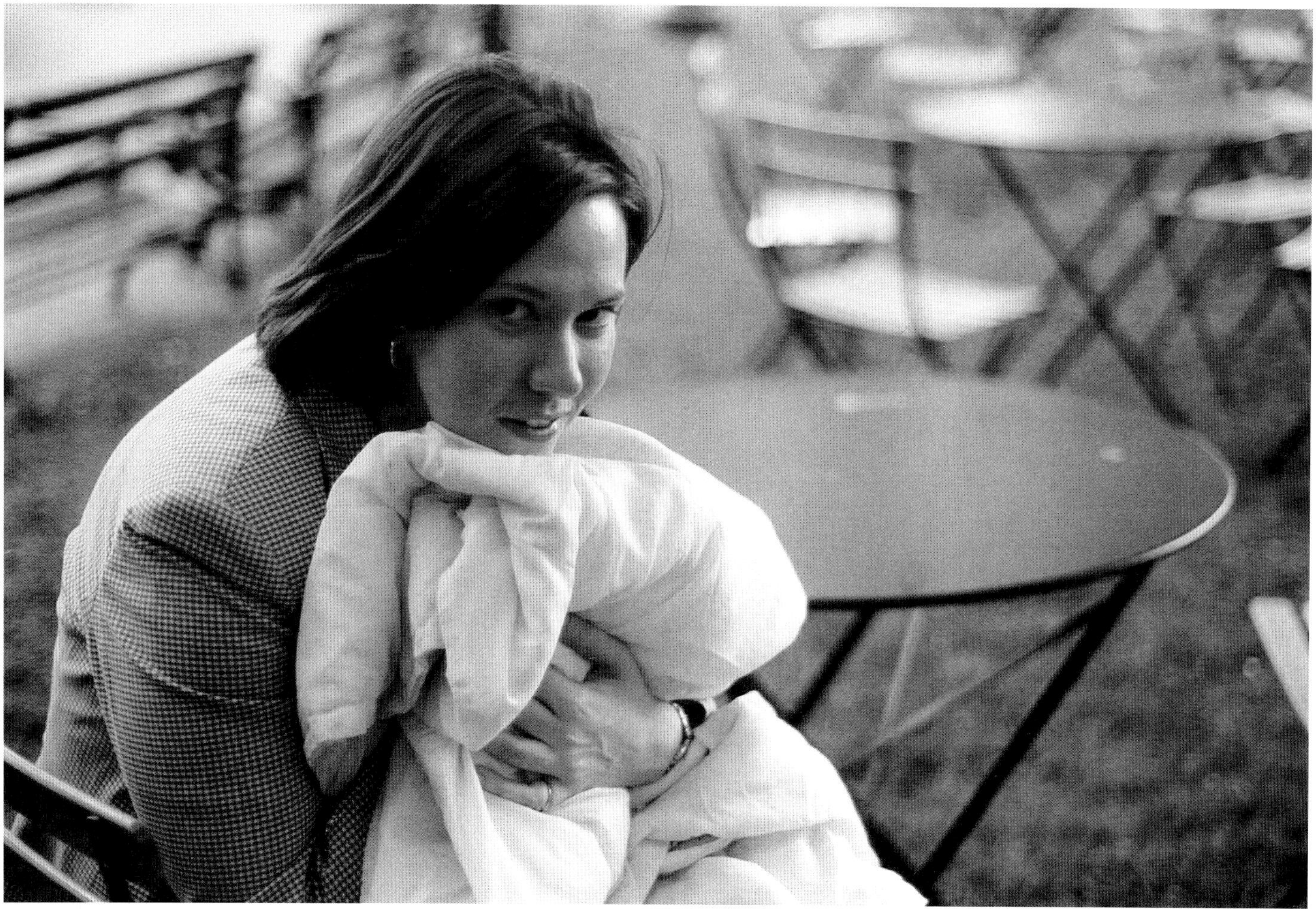

BOOKS

Perhaps it's not such a good thing, I think sometimes, that books are so important to my happiness. They give me realities alternate to my own, and is that dangerous, or short-changing someone, to need these other realities? But I've always felt this way. To learn to read was what I most wanted as a child, and reading is what I most want to do, often, now.

Truly, the lives in books have reached back into my own life and helped shaped it. They've made me braver, I know, and seeing characters in books has given me a way to see some of the people I know. And at the same time they've helped me treat my greediness - my one life never seems like enough, I want to know and feel more than I'll ever be allowed. From the safety of a couch, or a bus, I get to live through things I'd be too cowardly to choose for myself in my life.

In my tutoring program some people want to give the children only "relevant" books with stories and pictures out of their own experiences. Perhaps that's a good idea, but on the other hand, perhaps they want most to think about what it's like inside the two-story house with plush furniture and a maid named Amelia....

Karen Chatfield
IT Consultant

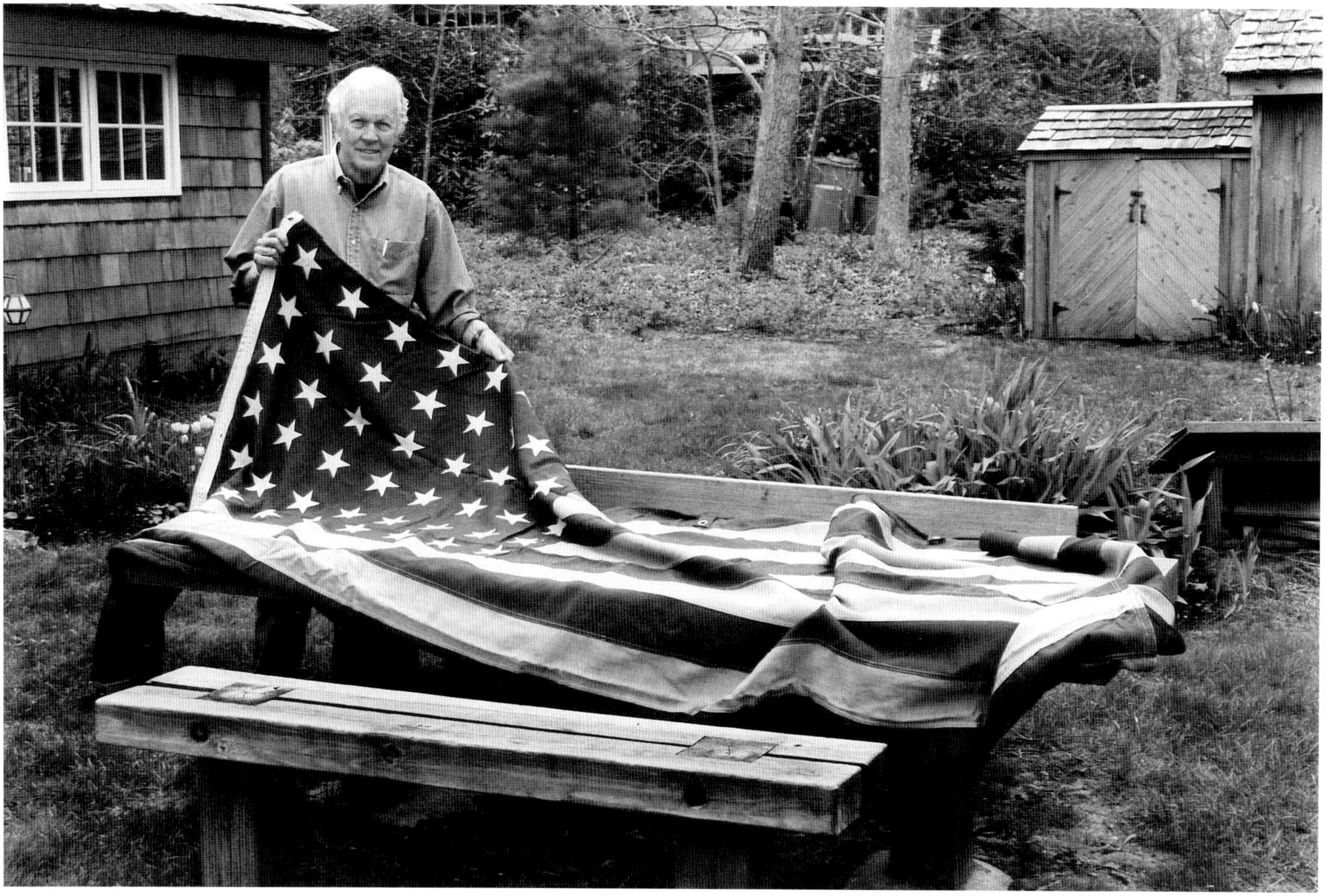

MY FATHER'S FLAG

If your house were burning down and you could rescue one possession, what would it be? For me it would be my father's flag. It is an old flag with only 48 stars.

My father, who was in the U.S. Navy, died serving his country in the last year of World War II. At that time he was in charge of New York City shore defense. When he suddenly died, I was only twelve years old and I tried to pretend that I didn't miss him, but now, fifty-two years later, I miss him a lot.

Although his career was in the navy, he had a passion and talent for art and design that directly influenced my own career decision to become a designer and illustrator. I often wonder what he would have thought of my work and wish I had him around to share my enthusiasm for the projects that I work on.

His last words were "How is David?" I think he said this because he saw in me the possible continuation of the things that he loved.

My father flew the flag outside our house as long as I can remember and after he died it became my job. Later, the same flag was laid over my father's coffin, since it was wartime and a military funeral.

This old flag, which I put out every Fourth of July just as he did, is not so much a symbol of our country for me, but a reminder of my father and of the short time we spent together.

David Stiles
Graphic Designer

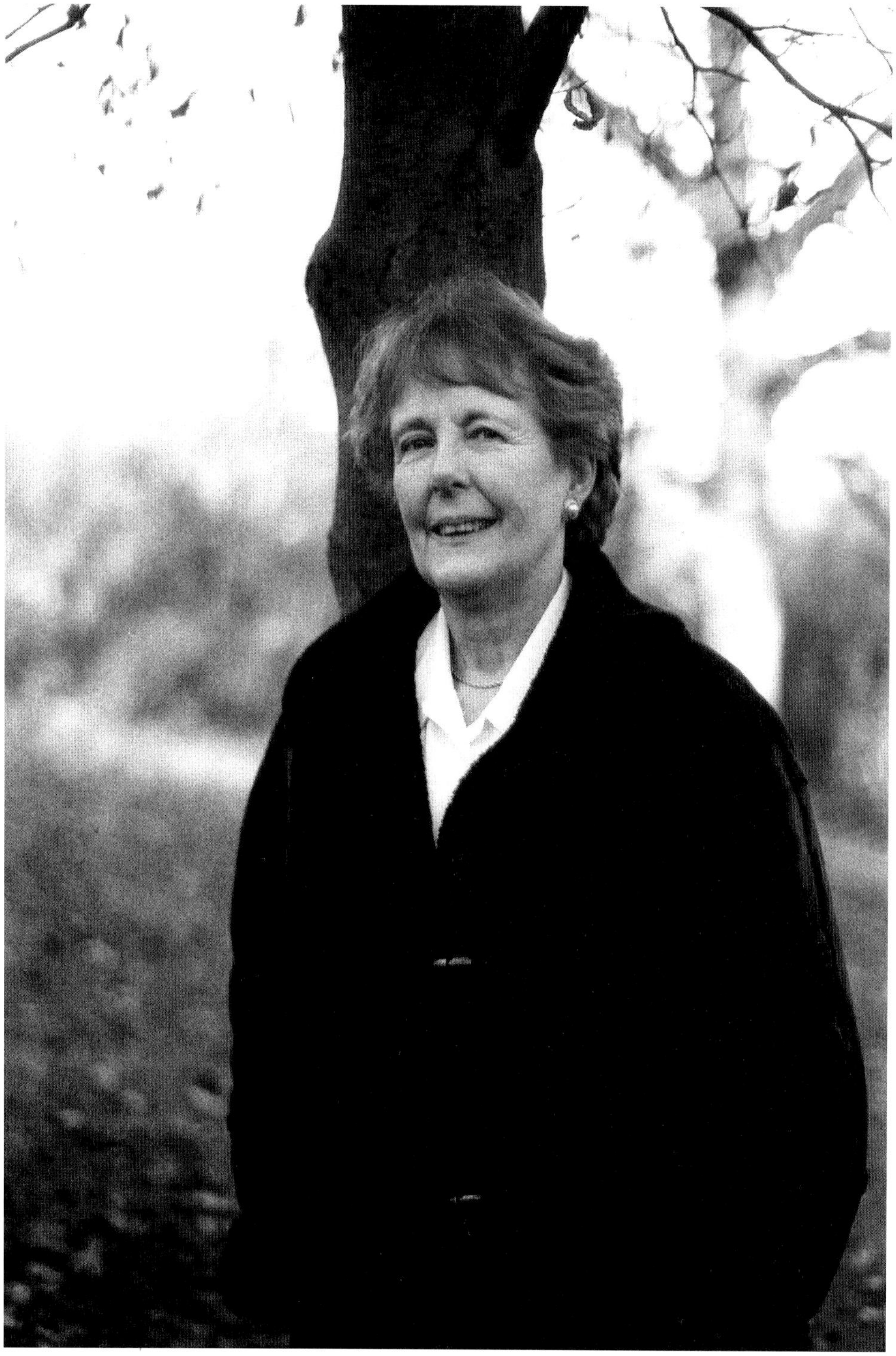

THE TREE

I have always loved trees which go through life with their head in the sky and their feet well anchored in the earth.

They face seasons, rustling in the breeze, moaning in the tempest, naked and proud in the cold of winter, generous with their shade during the hot season. Their branches resemble a Chinese print and their foliage is like a motherly embrace.

My tree, however, is unique in the world. Our son, no longer with us, wanted to put it in our garden. It is a purple beech which stands out in the surrounding greenery.

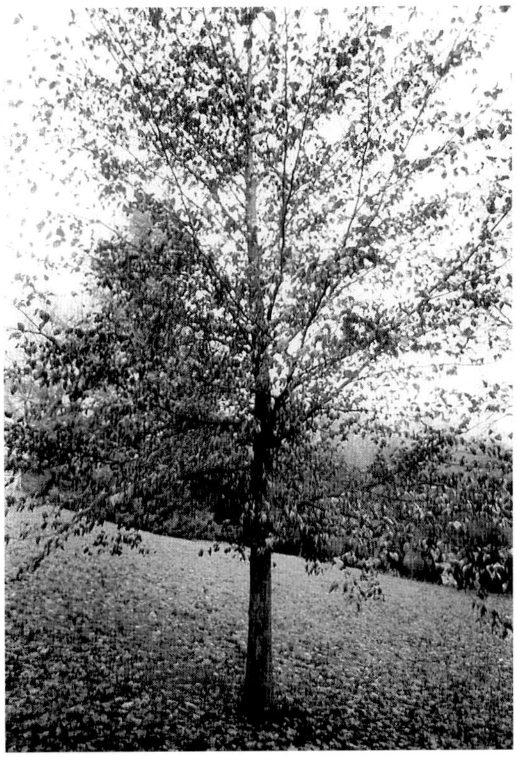

Though the leaves fade in the fall and become dry in the cold weather, they keep hanging all through winter, falling only a few days before the new golden brown buds appear.

All year long all strength and beauty, my tree is with me as a memory, as a friend.

Françoise Pellerin
Housewife

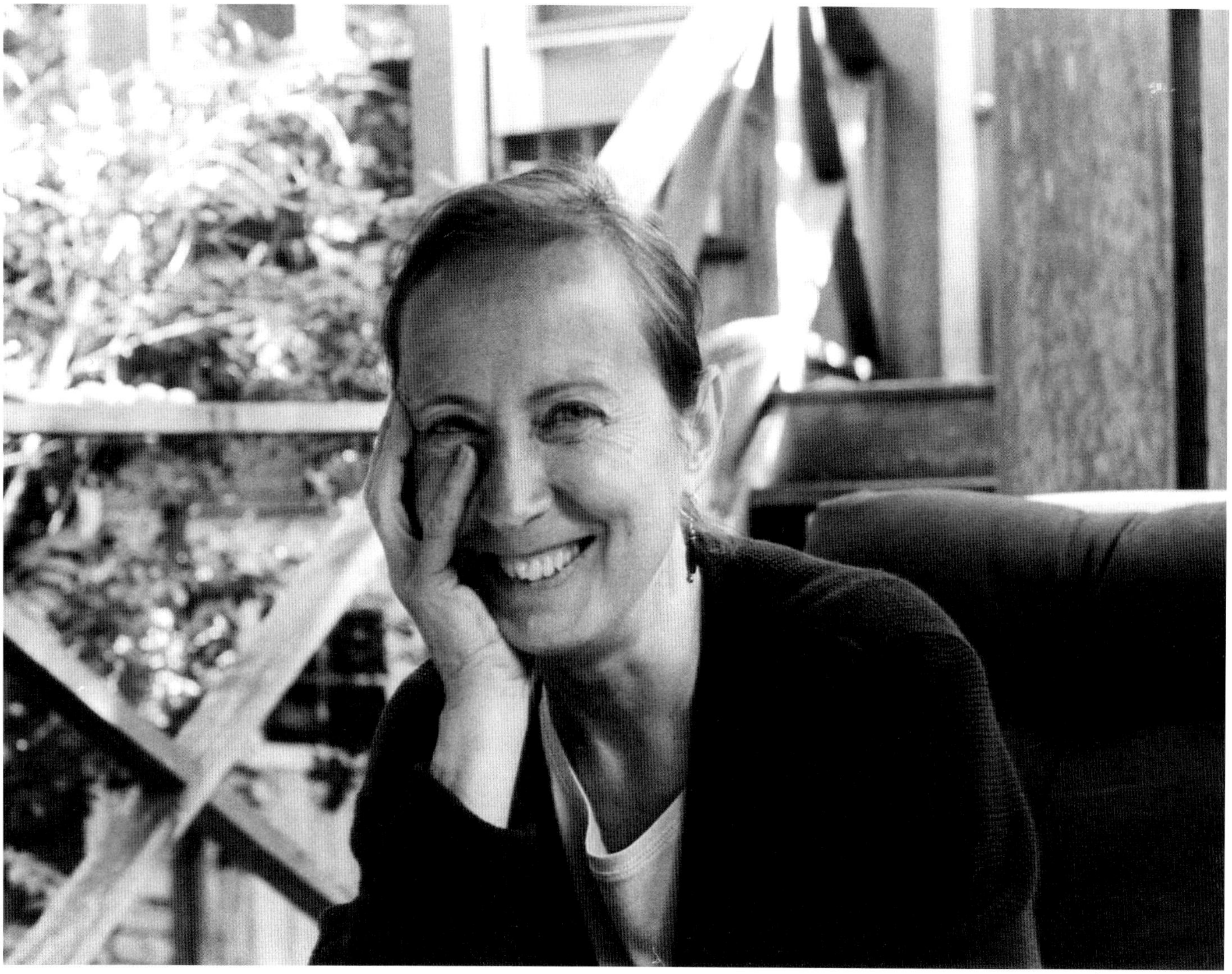
Courtesy of Gregory Black.

MY EARLY CHILDHOOD HOUSE

The house of my early childhood stood on a hill, strong and proud with its central flight of stairs and its many shuttered windows. A small garden was in the front; it was closed by an iron grid covered with ivy. My parents had rented the house at the very beginning of the war, thinking that it would be safer than in Paris.

I have only a vague memory of the interior: a small leather sofa on which my sisters and I did somersaults, my small wooden bed painted green, and a wood stove in the entrance hall.

On the other hand, I can visualize very clearly the small dirt garden with its water pump and its tiny roses climbing the flight of stairs. It was there that I used to play, and that, curious and full of innocence, I looked for the shrapnel shells which had fallen.

At the very top of the house was the dormer window of our nanny's room; we opened widely the window with its flower curtains smelling of her perfume, and discovered with excitement, far away beyond the Oise, a wide expanse of fields bathed in a very soft light. It is the light of Ile-de-France which has been so beautifully captured by Pissarro and Cézanne in their paintings of the small villages around, Auvers-sur-Oise, Le Valhermeil and Chaponval, our own village. Every time we opened the window, I was totally seduced by the beauty of those large spaces.

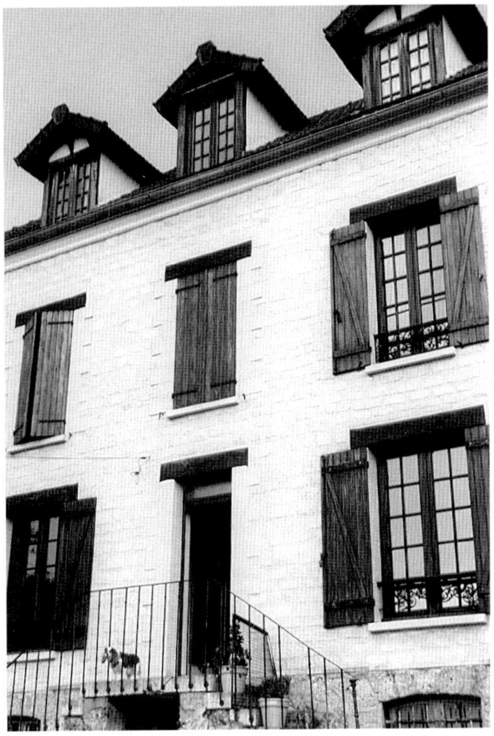

I spent my first years in this place and it is probably there that my love of nature, of vast spaces and my need for independence were born.

Our house, from which I used to escape to go and run in the fields above the hill, was for us a place of relative stability and quietness during the first years of the war. Soon we would have to go from one place to the other in order to escape danger.

Anne-Marie Cottenet Dannenberg
Photographer

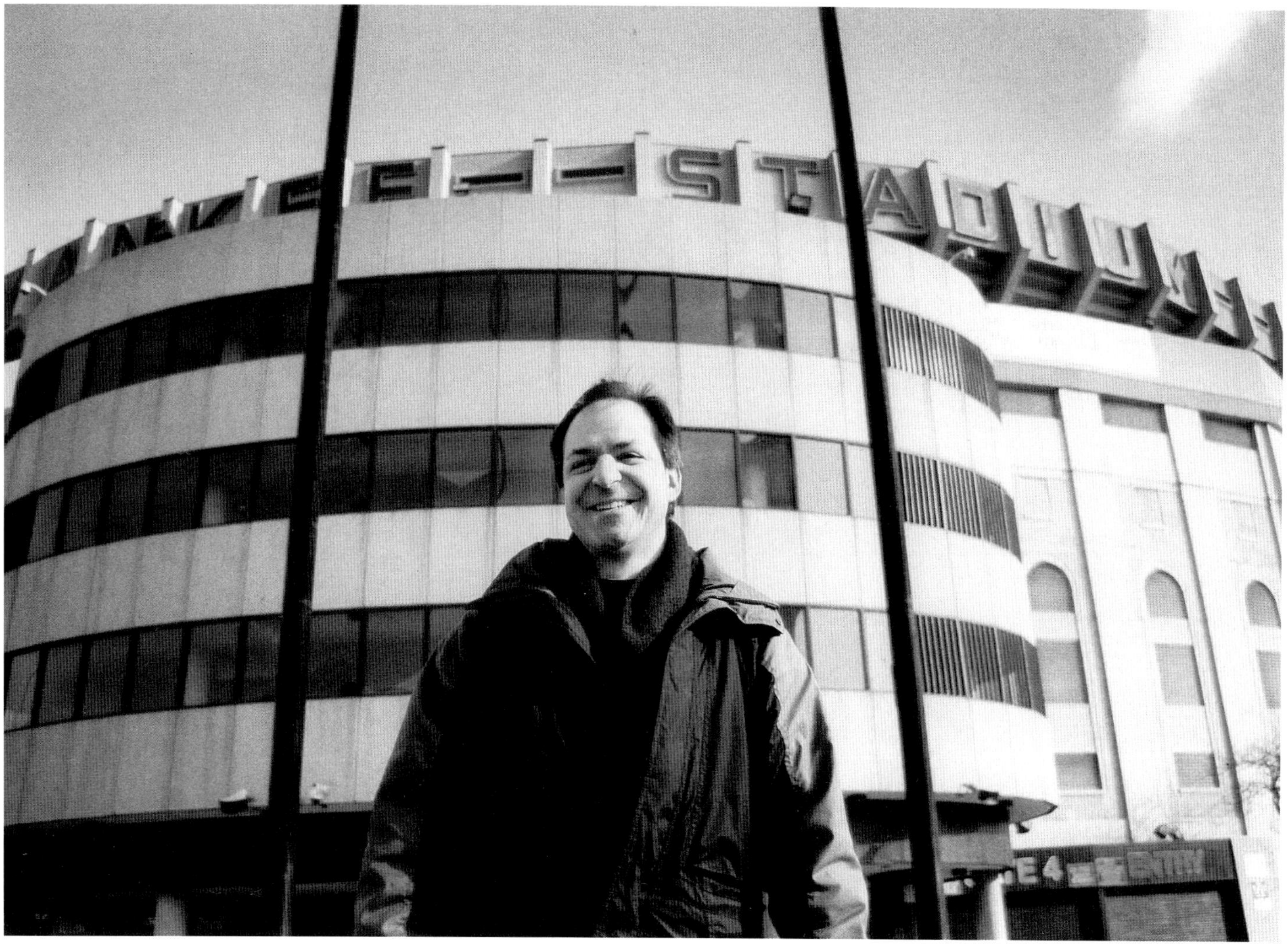

A FAN FOR LIFE

On a cool April night, in 1967, my father and I drove toward Yankee Stadium. I could see the stadium in the distance, bright lights gleaming in the darkest part of the South Bronx. "The House That Ruth Built", he would always say. I was seven years old. It seemed as though hours passed as we searched for a parking spot, then walked for blocks and blocks, the sound of the crowd growing louder and louder, the game had already started. As we entered the turnstiles, I clutched the torn tickets, ran up the concrete ramp, zig-zagging, the din of the crowd swelling with a crack of a bat. We approached the threshold to our spot in the stands, amazing! Bright lights, emerald green grass, the noise, the smell of roasted peanuts, hot dogs, beer and cigars. I recognized all of the players on the field from my baseball cards. I clutched my baseball glove, the glove that would accompany me to every game in hopes of snagging a foul ball. I never did. This was it, this was magic, this place would prove to be a refuge for me for years to come, a place where for a few hours at a time I would forget everything else in my life, this, after all was Yankee Stadium!

James Yacyshyn
Chef / Restaurant Owner

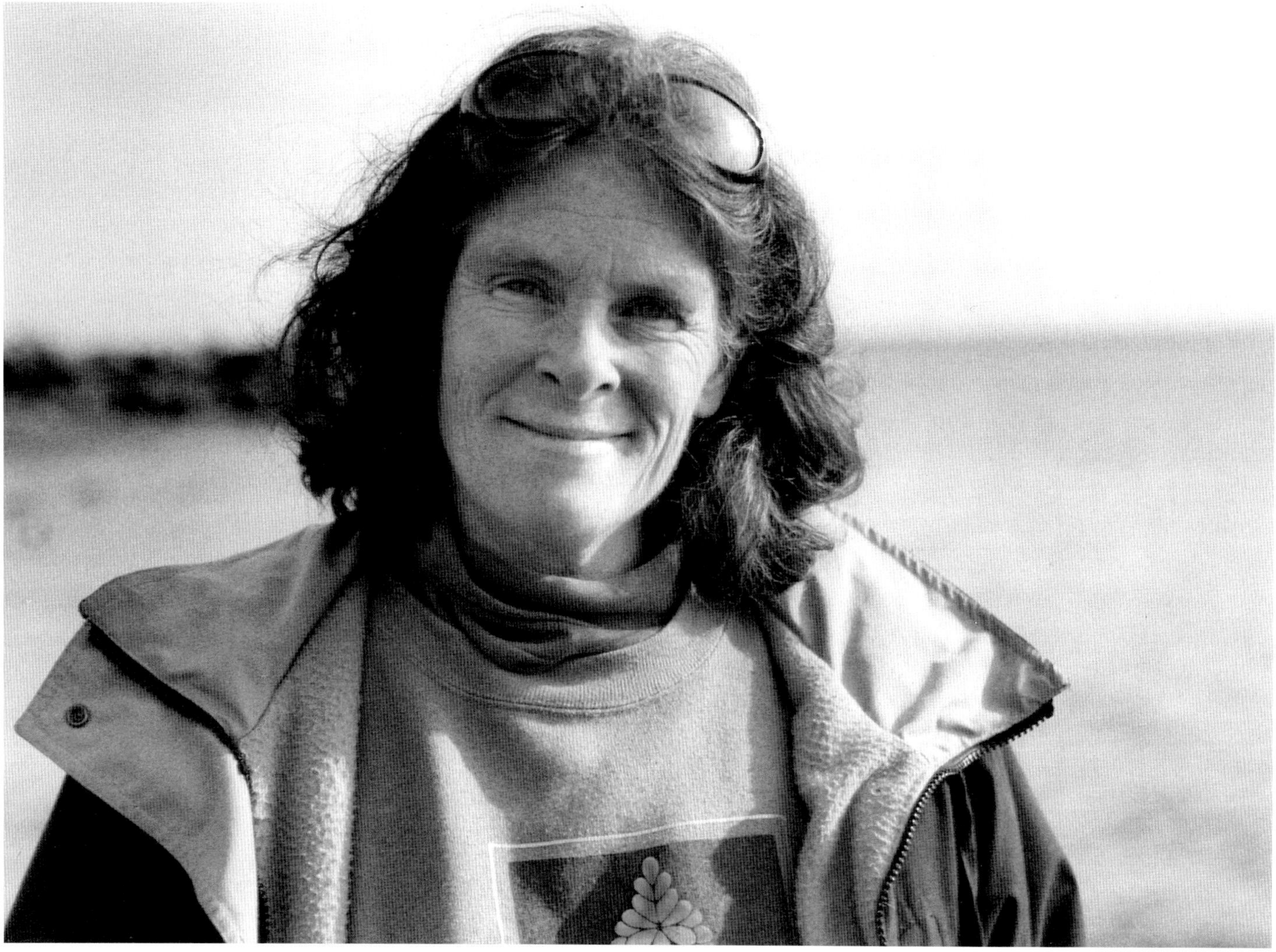

I wish to thank many friends for their help, numerous useful suggestions and support while I worked on the book project and most particularly Marie-Therese Brincard, Karen Chatfield, Madeleine Hage, Marjukka Kaminen, Fran Kaufman, Jean Toche, Hamid Tibouchi, Harold Wortsman and my husband Joseph Dannenberg. Without their support, help and encouragements, this book would not be here today...

AMCD

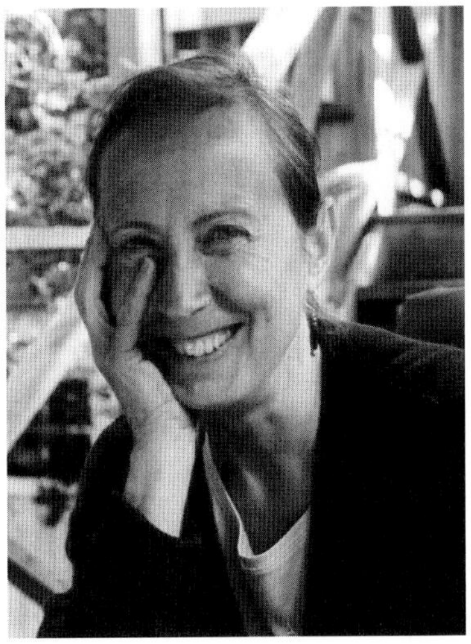